IN
Unexpected
PLACES

Where Jesus Christ Rules

IN
Unexpected
PLACES

Where Jesus Christ Rules

Tony Jasper
&
Myra Blyth

Marshall Pickering

Marshall Morgan and Scott
Marshall Pickering
3 Beggarwood Lane, Basingstoke, Hants RG23 7LP, UK

Copyright © 1988 Tony Jasper and Myra Blyth
First published in 1988 by Marshall Morgan and Scott Publications Ltd
Part of the Marshall Pickering Holdings Group
A subsidiary of the Zondervan Corporation

ISBN: 0 551 01626 4   098304

Text set in Baskerville by Brian Robinson, Buckingham
Printed in Great Britain by Cox and Wyman, Reading

Acknowledgements

Choice of material: Tony Jasper and Myra Blyth.
General introduction, worship orders, music choice, use of material suggestions: Tony Jasper.
Section commentaries: Myra Blyth.

Where there is no publisher or other source mentioned then copyright rests with the named writer. Tony Jasper and Myra Blyth apologise for any failure to acknowledge copyright and source. Some of their selection comes from material gathered over the years without sufficient record kept of derivation. Matters will be righted in any future edition. They trust unacknowledged sources will find pleasure in seeing their work included in this book. In most instances the given title of an extract has been devised for the purposes of this book.

Bowater, Chris: One With The Father, The Name Above All Names, The Spirit Comes As It Wills, No Defeat, from *Creative Worship*, Marshall Pickering.
Brokering, Herbert: Worship Happening, from *Concordia* (believed).
Corrymeela Community: Welcome.
Cotter, June: Awareness To, Prayer at Night, from *A Book For The Darkness*, Women's Press.
Free Church of Berkeley: Litany of Intercession, A Covenant of Peace, from *A Liberation Prayer Book*, Morehouse-Marlow Co. Inc. Wilton, Connecticut, U.S.A.
Galliard: There You Will Find Him.
Gaunt, Alan, He Does So Much, Praise God, He Makes All Things New, To Encounter The Living God, So Marvellous, from *New Prayers for Worship*, The Preachers Press.

General Globe of Ministries, United Methodist Church, U.S.A.: Yo So Ella, from *Things Hoped For*.

Gregory, John: When You Started The Universe, from *New Church Praise*.

Habel, Norman: Someday Soon, from *Interrobang, Prayers and Shouts*, The Lutterworth Press, Philadelphia: Fortress Press.

Hawkins, Maureen: The Miracle, from *Creative Writing by Black Women In Britain*, (Eds. Rhonda Cobham and Merle Collins), Women's Press.

Hays, Edward: A Fool's Prayer.

Hedges, Graham: If Only, from *Buzz/21st Century Christian, Contemporary Prayers for Christian Worship*.

Hewitt, William: The Spirit Directs, Where New Winds Blow, See The Kingdom, from The Way Magazine.

Hill, David: Lord We Praise You, from the musical *Crows and Methodists*.

Hornsby, Sarah: My Sister And My Friend, Love Prayer to Jesus, from *Nicaraguense*, Marshall Pickering.

Iona Community: God and Man and Woman.

Johnson, Amryl: Dying In The Street, from *Creative Writing by Black Women in Britain*, Eds. Rhonda Cobham and Merle Collins), Women's Press.

Keen, Sam: Hot Faith, from *To A Dancing God*, Harper & Row.

Mallison, John: Prayer, from *Creative Ideas*, Renewal Publications (Australia).

Methodist Church (UK), Overseas Division: God Is Alive, His Active and Healing Peace, from *Prayer Power*.

Micklem, Caryl: As Best We Can, SCM Press.

Morena, Naomi Littebear: Age Irrelevant, Gentle Angry People, Alliance of Radical Methodists.

Morley, Janet: For Wholeness, from *Celebrating Women*, MOW.

Motive Magazine U.S.A.: The Thirty-Seventh Parallel.

Phillips, Betsy Fisher: O God I Am Chained, Images, from *Women In Transition*, Women's Press.

Resources For Youth Ministry, Board of Youth Ministry,

Lutheran Church, U.S.A.: A Morning Prayer Of The Kingdom, from *Worship Resource Book*.

Samartha, Stanley, J.: The Pillar of Salt Speaks, WCC, Geneva.

Sanchez, Sonia: Present, from *Generations*, Karnak House.

Shea, John: Together With Him, from *The Hour of the Unexpected*, Tabor Publishing.

Short, Raymond: Making Himself Known, Methodist Church (UK).

Sojourner's Peace Ministry, Washington D.C.: Always, Thanks, My People, I Am Your Security, The True Peace.

Springsteen, Anne: For The Right Words, from *It's Me, O Lord*, 1970, Concordia Publishing House.

Stewart, Carole: Don't Call Me Mama, Women's Press.

Taize Community: The Holy Spirit, The All-Embracing Spirit.

Taylor, Cecily: Walking On Water, from *Christian Celebration*, Mayhew McCrimmon.

Wahlberg, Rachel C.: Women's Friend, from *No Longer Strangers*, WCC, Geneva

Walsh Ken: Last Night I Saw, from *Sometimes I Weep,* SCM.

WCC, Geneva: Lord Of All; Praise; Flat Day on the Metro, from *Consultation in Zurich*.

Weiser, Conrad: Strings, Wires, Ropes and Chains, from *Dancing All The Dances, Singing All The Songs.* Fortress Press.

Word Publishing: To Every Generation.

Other permissions according to name of writer, details where relevant can be obtained from the compilers of this book.

Contents

Introduction

In Unexpected Places follows our last collection *At All Times And In All Places*. This new book appears not because we had too much left over last time, but rather because there is so much exciting material continually appearing—material which we have used in our worship services, and in religious gatherings of all kinds, shapes and sizes.

We recoil at the view that we are trying to be trendy. Nothing is further from our mind; but if some people think this is our aim, there is little we can do about it. We are not against time-honoured words, sentences, phrases, beautiful English, set orders, historic ways of celebrating God, His Son, His Holy Spirit. We do not belong to the band of Christians who arrogantly believe Christian life and witness have been in the dark ages ever since the last words of Scripture were penned. Nor do we subscribe to those contemporary worship gatherings that are marked by paucity of thought but well endowed with excitement and emotion. We are certainly for silence, and equally for a whole panoply of material that stretches our minds and thoughts, that can lift us beyond, and to the mountain top, and yet can also enable us to follow His footsteps through the grime and dirt of everyday life in the twentieth century.

In the previous collection we were commended by the reviewer in the *Church Times* for our inclusion of the powerful summary of worship that first appeared in *No Longer Strangers* by Iben Gjerding and Katherine Kinnamon: we repeat it here simply because it still excites us:

* to recall and reflect on the saving acts of God recorded in scripture;
* to find and celebrate the presence of God in everyday life;
* to lay before God their deepest fears, joys and hopes;

* to dare to acknowledge the holy within their lives and within the ordinary things of daily experience;
* to find hope through the goodness of God within their personal and communal lives;
* to give thanks for God's gracious love, expressed through Jesus Christ.

Within this volume there is, we believe, material suitable for many occasions, material which celebrates our overall theme of The Kingdom. A glance at the book's basic outline will show that after some basic underpinning of Trinitarian theology we explore The Kingdom in various ways. Christians try hard to contend with the idea that the Kingdom of God is neither simply here (on earth) or there (in heaven) but is present in part. Here, we explore the discovery of the Kingdom in the life of the Church and the world as well as in each other. The Kingdom, in the first place, can be sought. We can then endeavour to extend the Kingdom, while the evidence of our Kingdom membership will be shown in our lives: in giving and receiving, in love shown to the unloved. Finally, we must look forward to the Kingdom completed: 'Come, Lord Jesus!'

As in *At All Times And In All Places* there is considerable variation in material: in style, language, and level of spiritual awareness; and without, we hope, condescending, we do suggest that a general Christian gathering is an incredible mix and at very least we are aware that 'words' spoken and read constitute for some these days almost an alien form of communication. But even the most difficult and seemingly obtuse piece of writing can at least be imbued by the reader, actor, whatever you choose to call the role, with a spirit and image that will convey the overall mood of the extract, and the response of the hearing gatherings will heighten this sense.

We take extracts from numerous Christian sources, ranging from charismatic to areas that might be described as 'grey'. But does not the Spirit blow in unexpected ways from unusual directions? We were particularly thrilled that the 'mix' in our previous volume found a home in many different places.

However, there are some areas where we are very clear. For the most part, we trust we have not perpetuated 'maleness' to the exclusion of all else. We have deliberately ensured that women writers have been greatly used, and we shall be disturbed if exclusive language is seen. Some prayers and meditations clearly come from women seeking a new articulation of Christian truth that is being undertaken from the perspective of women; and some would say, as have Janice Morley and Hannah Ward in their introduction to the much recommended *Celebrating Women* collection, that 'some of the hidden insights of women are only beginning to be expressed'. But we hope you will not find this contribution in the least odd, or even be aware of it; after all, it should be as natural as air.

We have aimed for a 'world' feel; and most certainly that our content should cover areas of life particularly relevant to people of the so-called 'pop age', and to all of us living in a world marked by mis-use of resources, power complexes that take and give little, the bastions of racism, numerous injustices and a seeming lack of willingness to search for justice and righteousness; a world of unemployment, sexual harassment and questioning, AIDS; of consumerism, ecological abuses, war machines, political lies and expedient politicians, and a general sense of 'lostness' and of the 'desert'. This is our world, and these are some of the themes which find their way into the book's content.

In some ways both of us have an unease about directing how or in what ways this material may be presented, felt and experienced. We would see people coming to the text and sensing how it applies in their circumstances; for everything here must live or die accordingly, and we have no idea where, when and how our collection will be explored and given flesh. And by giving some guide as to methods of using the book, we may fall into the dire strait of the drama producer who directs so rigidly that a state of dependency is established and creativity stifled. Yes, we have given *some* ideas—persuaded by brute force, the empty room, typewriter, table, locked door and threats that there must be results in sixteen hours! We have been convinced that some suggestions will help; but please do not imagine that we are offering anything more, and certainly, unless you are 'up against it', just use our jottings as a voice among many.

The same attitude should govern the ten outline services. Here, especially, there are so many unknown factors, the most obvious being the room or building, from décor to light to sound to seating to space to overall ambience and, not least, colour, symbol and image; and finally the make-up of the gathering itself.

Above all, we would not seek to discourage people from developing their own liturgies, prayers and meditations.

We are not interested in 'casual' worship, where anything goes. The words we have used have not just arrived—they have come from communities and individuals who have sweated and toiled, who have given birth to their thoughts from risking faith. True dependence on God does not come from a mumbled 'yes', as though it is one option among many; it derives, like true freedom, from the cultivation of inner awareness, a sense of God's closeness, the reality of His nearness, an awareness of His greatness from knowing He is worthy of a greater love and service than we can ever offer or understand. And although we are not suggesting these are foolproof criteria for giving birth to promising new material, we ask you to wonder how much sweat and pain have been experienced in your group as you have battled for fresh understanding, new methods and ways, words and none, of celebrating the Faith. Should the answer be 'None', then we suggest you try again! We can assure you—it don't come easy! Any more than in compiling a collection such as this—it isn't a case of slapping together extracts culled from cupboards and drawers and rushing through any seemingly new(ish) book on our shelves or those of a religious bookshop.

Please write and let us know if this collection has been of use in your worship situation: tell us, and give us a chance to look at what you have produced.

Note on introductory material to the various extracts:
In most cases there is suggestion how a group or whole gathering might make use of this material. However, much of it can be said by one person, if it seems best that the familiar role of the 'one' leader of worship should be enacted. The statements preceding most sections are for general reflection or to form the basis of discussion in a 'worship' theme gathering.

Worship Notes and Thoughts

Nine theses on the place of worship in the life of a local congregation

1. Worship in the New Testament is not ritually or ceremonially defined or described. But it did 'happen' when the Church 'assembled'. This was sometimes a daily event; sometimes weekly. Annual Jewish feasts continued either to be celebrated or taken over in different form.
2. The 'worship-happening' in the early Church generally took one of two forms, which finally came together:
   (1) a teaching, instructional session, and
   (2) a common meal, according to apostolic example. Both these forms involved singing, praying, meeting and some ecstatic behaviour.
3. As the post-apostolic Church began to take definite shape and form around officers and creeds, its assembly also began to assume a pattern: Word and Sacrament. The underlying meaning of the pattern continued to be the presence of Christ in the body, the body of believers, and in his word, the word of scripture, sermon and sacrament. The assembly was the central act and reality of the Church.
4. The Eastern Orthodox Church has preserved both the pattern and the meaning, with special emphasis on worship as an anticipation of the glory of the Kingdom.
5. The Western Church, by the time of the Reformation, had lost the pattern with the disappearance at the Sacrament (Mass) of the teaching ministry (which occurred elsewhere). The meaning had taken on more cultic and individualistic significance with heavy emphasis upon sin, and salvation in heaven.

6. The Protestant Reformers, Luther, Calvin and Cranmer saw worship as the central event of the Church's life, and sought to restore the unity of Word and Sacrament. This program failed. Zwingli's pattern of a Sunday teaching service with an occasional sacramental occasion for renewed personal rededication and fellowship succeeded.

7. The post-Reformation situation resulted in the Roman Church keeping the Sacrament and the Protestants, the sermon; but the two halves of worship, without one another, became caricatures of themselves.

8. The renewal of the Church today inevitably involves the pattern, meaning and style of its worship, because its 'presence' in the world, its mission, is dependent upon its being a body, its corporate existence.

9. In the last analysis the Church's only tool for evangelism is itself.

Rev Dr Horace T. Allen, Jr

What prayer is

Prayer is listening. It is being still to know that God is God.

Prayer is contemplation. It is thinking about God in long periods of silence. It is deep thought and meditation with expectation.

Prayer is a fleeting thought directed to God.

Prayer is a deep unuttered desire within a human heart.

Prayer is talking to God. It is a 'child' talking to a loving Heavenly Father.

Prayer is an instantaneous cry for help.

Prayer is conversation. It is both talking and listening.

Prayer is communion. It is a meeting between two who are in love. The Eternal Source of all Agape Love reaches down to touch a human being who makes an inadequate response.

Prayer is the faltering words of a person with no faith probing for God of Whom he is uncertain, in a search for reality and meaning.

Prayer is a grain of faith moving a person to ask and expect miracles.

Prayer is breathing, spiritually. It is 'the Christian's vital breath, the Christian's native air'.

Prayer is affirming God. It is bringing delight to God—making Him glad.

Prayer is saying 'I'm sorry' to God and asking for grace not to repeat our failure.

Prayer is asking forgiveness for God's sake as well as for our sake.

Prayer is bringing the big challenges and responsibilities of life to God and receiving His divine enablement.

Prayer is having faith to bring the mundane 'non-events', the routine, small things of life to God believing He cares for the insignificant 'lilies of the field', 'the birds of the air', and how much more for us.

Prayer is both asking and receiving.

Prayer is bringing to God my deep concern for those who are near to me, my family, my close circle of friends.

Prayer is acknowledging my membership in this global village and praying as specifically as I can for my brothers and sisters in this world who are unknown to me by name.

Prayer is laying before God a concern for our enemies.

Prayer is the way to inner serenity—it is the calm found in the eye of the hurricane, not an escape from the turmoils of life.

Prayer is where I meet my risen Lord—where I learn to know Him and the power of His resurrection.

Prayer is the child's simplest form of communication with God.

Prayer is an art which none of the saints felt they had fully mastered.

Prayer is praying when we don't feel like talking with God because we believe He is always loving us, always listening, always wanting to bless us with His grace and love.

Prayer is a family conversing with God. It is the deepest of human fellowship.

Prayer is keeping my contribution short when praying with

others to help their concentration and giving them a fair
share of the conversation with our Father.

Prayer is honesty and openness with God, both when I pray
in solitude and when I pray with others.

Prayer is work.

Prayer is believing the 'Holy Spirit within us is actually
praying for us in those agonising tongues which never
find words'.

Prayer is where our hope is confirmed, our faith strength-
ened, our love enriched, our authenticity increased, and a
depth and sensitivity given to life which can be found
nowhere else.

Worship

'Anywhere—Everywhere'

In times of personal crisis people often go into a church
looking for God, hoping in God, to find help. In one sense
they are right: God can be found in a church and where
God is there is hope. In another sense their action is
unnecessary for God is Everywhere and sometimes more
powerfully present in the most Unexpected Places. C. S.
Lewis first encountered God on the top of a double decker
bus. Thomas Merton, the Trappist monk, first encountered
God or at least an interest in God in conversation with an
Indian Guru. So clearly there is no accounting for when or
where.

If, as it is said, 'God is nearer to us than we are to
ourselves', why go looking?—God who is everywhere
present has already found us!

To read: Psalm 136, 'Hide and Seek'
The Psalmist makes it clear that even if we wanted to run
away from God's presence we cannot. The fact is, God is,
even in the depths of Sheol.

To Reflect: 'Sometimes I do not know' (page 62)
God belongs everywhere and so do our prayers. This whole

book is based on that conviction and not least in this prayer which frees us to worship and pray wherever we may find ourselves.

Worship happening

Seat someone on a high stool, tell as a story.

The minister was on vacation.
The congregation held a happening.
They gathered in the parking lot . . . set off firecrackers . . . ate popcorn . . . sang a Thanksgiving hymn . . . folded their hands . . . said Amen seven times . . . walked in single file . . . took off their shoes in the vestibule . . . were blindfolded . . . heard the Scriptures read . . . applauded for five minutes . . . looked each other in the eye . . . took turns looking out the door through binoculars . . . turned on the rock 'n' roll station . . . read Psalm 23 with jazz on loud . . . read the Gospel out loud together . . . said three Yes's after each sentence . . . went swimming . . . touched breast and brow with the sign of the cross each time they entered the pool . . . bought the daily newspaper . . . rode the ferris wheel, shouting the headlines until the wheel stopped . . . fed each other ice cream . . . struck each other three times . . . screamed for help . . . shook hands . . . threw seed into a garden . . . chanted the Magnificat . . . skipped seven stones across the water . . . each time saying one of the seven last words of the cross . . . threw dice . . . chose up seven sides . . . had a relay race carrying a Bible on their heads . . . raced each other to the cars, praying the Lord's Prayer all the way . . . phoned each other upon arriving home . . . pronounced the Benediction upon each other.
Lord, I was in charge.
What shall I say to the minister when he returns?

Herbert Brokering

This American piece needs only a few changes in words, and is best enacted!

God, Jesus, Holy Spirit

God and me

Heart stopping
breath holding
cover my head,
bare my feet.
God is here.

Heart stopping,
breath holding
sink to my knees.
God is here.

Heart stopping,
breath holding,
He touches me
warm fire explodes
singingly
inside my head.
God is here.

Heart stopping
breath holding,
I dare to look
at the face of God.
Oh joy—
He
knows
me.

Beth Webb

Use several voices with all voices combining for the words 'God is here'.

To see God

If we could see God,
we wouldn't be lolling lazy in pews
or thinking about the vicar's ears,
or whether our shoes hurt.
If we could see God.

If we could see God
we would not dare breathe
with the joy and the wonder of it.
Then comes the deep silence.
Then the great shout.
We would all become as translucent
as rainbows
stretching up to the very sky with joy.
If—
we could see God.

If we could see God,
but we can't;
so we shift on the hard pews,
wondering why that woman
lets her boy pick his nose.
And then we go home.
Pity we can't see God
—like Thomas did.

Beth Webb

*As with 'God and me' try this with several different voices and have
everyone in the line-up say the last line of each stanza.*

God—always present

Leader: God is here. He is now.

All say this modern version of Psalm 98:

Men and women have proclaimed God's praises throughout the ages,

Now it is our turn to worship the Lord and announce God's presence and His loving concern for the inhabitants of this world.

His power is as great today as it ever was. He continues to reign over His universe—and the creatures that move in this world.

God alone is the true God.

God offers to all men and women His salvation.

God is close to His sons and daughters, His servants.

Let us express this joy. With voice and musical instruments, with lovely melodies and joyful sounds, let us proclaim the glory of God.

Let us fill our homes and our churches, our places of learning, our factories and market-places, even the streets of our town and cities—with the sounds of celebration.

Pause, pause.

All say: GOD IS HERE, GOD IS NOW.

The Sanctus

Four men say, then four women say, then all eight say:
  Holy is God
The gathering says:
  Means God is a mystery.
Four men say, then four women say, then all eight say:
  Holy is God
The gathering says:
  Means God wins the victory.
Four women say, four men say, then all eight say:
  Holy is God
The gathering says:
  Means God joins humanity.
All say:
  Overwhelm Him with praise.

Females to say: Holy is God Who has forces flying everywhere.
Males to say: Holy is God Who has life leaping everywhere.

Females to say: Holy is God Who has light dawning everywhere.
All say: Overwhelm Him with praise.
Repeat, but reverse female-male lines.

All say:
  Jesus our King Who is coming in the name of God,
  Jesus our King Who is coming by the will of God,
  Jesus our King Who is coming as the man of God,
Male voices: Overwhelm Him with praise,
Female voices: Overwhelm Him with praise,
All say: OVERWHELM HIM WITH PRAISE.

We begin

Voice: We begin
Response: In the Name of the Father, the Son and the Holy
            Spirit.
V: We begin
R: As we began;
            In the Name of the Father, the Son and the Holy
            Spirit.
V: We begin
R: As creation began;
            As all of life began;
            When water, Word and Spirit came together
            To create new life, a new world, new people.
V: We begin
R: As we began
            When we were created anew
            By water, Word, and Spirit
            In the Name of the Father, Son and Holy Spirit.

Opening responses

Leader: In the beginning, when it was very dark, God said,
          'Let there be light.'
People: AND THERE WAS LIGHT.
                The sign of light—a candle is lit.

Leader: In the beginning, when it was very quiet, the Word was with God.

People: AND WHAT GOD WAS, THE WORD WAS.

> *The sign of the word—a Bible is opened.*

Leader: When the time was right, God sent his Son.

People: HE CAME AMONG US, HE WAS ONE OF US.

> *The sign of the Son—a cross is placed.*

It is He

Thou art the great God—he who is in heaven.
Thou art the Hunter who hunts for souls.
Thou art the great Mantle which covers us.
Thou art he whose hands are with wounds.

Xhosa Christian in South Africa

Say as a gathering, or hear it said by an African who can say and tell of a suffering with Christ.

The Lord God

Leader: High over all the nations is the Lord God!

All: His glory is greater than the heavens!

Leader: Who is like the Lord our God?

All: Blessed be the name of God, henceforth and forever!

He is to be praised

Minister: Praise the Lord.

Together say: The Lord's name be praised.

Minister: Praise the Lord.

Together say: Glory to God, glory,
O praise Him, Alleluia!
Glory to God, glory,
O praise the name of the Lord.

Minister: Almighty God, Father, Son and Holy Spirit,

Together say: We praise you for all good gifts we have

received and for your promise of peace and joy
to all people; blessed be your wonderful name
forever and forever. Amen.

All things are His

The gathering:
Yours is the Kingdom, Yours is the power,
Yours is the glory for evermore, for evermore, for
evermore.
Yours is the Kingdom, the power and the glory for
evermore.

Repeat, using (1) female voice; (2) male voices; (3) the gathering.

Lord of all

Voice 1: O Supreme Lord of the Universe,
You fill and sustain everything around us;
With the touch of your hand you turned
chaos into order, darkness into light.
Voice 2: Unknown energies you hid in the heart of matter,
From you bursts forth the splendour of the sun,
and the mild radiance of the moon.
Stars and planets without number you set in
ordered movement.
Voice 3: You are the source of the fire's heat and the wind's
might,
of the water's coolness and the earth's stability.
Deep and wonderful are the mysteries of your
creation.
All: We adore you, you are beyond all form!
You give form to everything, Lord of all creation.
Voice 4: God of all salvation,
You formed us in your own image.
Female: You created us male and female,
Male: You created us male and female,
Female: you willed our union and harmony.

Male: You entrusted the earth to our care
Female: and promised your blessing to all descendants.
Male: You gave us the spirit of discernment to know you,
Female: the power of speech to celebrate your glory,
Male: the strength of love to give ourselves in joy to you.
Female: In this wondrous way, O God,
Male: you called us to share
Female: in your own being,
Male: your own knowledge,
Female: your own bliss.
All: In the Oneness of the Supreme Spirit,
through Christ who unites all things in his fullness
we and the whole creation give to you
honour and glory, thanks and praise,
worship and adoration,
now and in every age, for ever and ever. Amen.

Glory be to the Father . . .

Leader: Glory be to the Father, through the Son, in Holy
Spirit.
All: Not as people worthy but looking only to your
goodness so we lift up our voices to you, father.
You are the maker, lover, and keeper of all life,
You are above us and beneath us, around us, within
us.
You are in the world, sustaining, moulding, above
all loving.
In Christ above all we have seen your will and love at
work within the world of time
and yet not even Jesus Christ can exhaust your love.
We rejoice before you this day,
Here, every time we gather, we cry 'He is risen'.
May empty hearts, empty heads, hands with nothing
to do, feet with nowhere to go never be ours.

Making himself known

Leader: Lord God, infinite Father, great Creator, compassionate Saviour,
All: We are known to you, make yourself known to us.
Leader: Lord Jesus Christ, Son of the Living God,
All: Come to us, speak your word to each heart.

Leader: Gracious God, source of all mercy and hope,
All: Give us life in your name.
Leader: God of love who gave us your Son,
All: Enable us to respond to your gift.

Leader: Lord Jesus Christ, come to save a fallen race,
All: Without you, we are helpless.
Leader: Lord Jesus Christ, incarnation of God's mercy,
All: Through you may we receive:
Health—
Wholeness,
Salvation.

Leader: Holy Spirit of God we need your help,
All: Increase and establish our faltering faith.
Leader: Holy Spirit, convince us,
All: Guide us into all the truth which is in Jesus Christ.

A Celebration in Words and Music

How great you are

Say standing, with enthusiasm and energy.

We thank you, God!
We want to tell the world
what you have done;
your wonderful works.
We praise you, God!
We remember our beginnings

and celebrate belonging
together in your world.
We trust you, God!
You are still our help.
We go forward in faith
remembering all you have done.

Paraphrase of Psalm 105:1–5

God for us

All: We name you, Lord our God,
and we bless you now
on this day which you have given us.
We adore you,
overwhelmed or serene,
alienated or rebellious,
believing and not believing
at the same time.
You are a God of living people.
You were not ashamed to be our God,
eternal and faithful
in life and death,
in good times and in bad.
Amen.

Huub Oosterhuis

God of all

God of Moses, saved in the river;
God of Israel, freed from Egypt, freed from the desert;
God of the slain Lamb, powerless Lion of Judah;
God of Brazil, of the millions exploited by the black magic of
  growth;

God of Mexico, of the ambivalence of the revolution;
God of New York, London, Paris, Moscow (*add as thought fit*),
    of disappointment and of new life;
God of theologians, deceived by the wind of doctrine;
God of the bureaucrats, nervously searching for new
    programmes;
God of Africa, of a growing church in a land of exploitation;
God of the religious people, caught in the projection of their
    own mind;
God of the conservatives, of the burning desire to save
    souls;
God of the liberals, dreaming of reform;
God of the radicals, dreaming of revolution;
God of the artists, creativity of man;
God of the technocrats, enslaved to the power they hold;
God of the exploiters, love of power;
God of the Christians between faith and unfaith;
God of those who have never heard of Jesus Christ;
God of those who have heard of Christ but see only his
    people;
God of us—God of all men and women,
    surprise us anew with your faithfulness, save us today!

Have five groups of four: each person says a line. At
completion of four lines all four people say the last line of this
prayer. At the end all twenty say together the last line; then
the whole gathering.

God is alive

Leader*: Because of every evidence, in the world, in the
    Church and in our own lives, that God is alive and at
    work:
One half of gathering: Let us bless the Lord!
Other half of gathering: Praise his name!
Leader: Because in so many parts of the world the Church is
    growing in numbers, confidence and courage:
Gathering response as above.

Leader: Because through the spirit we have fellowship with his people in every part of the earth:

Gathering response as above.

Leader: Because He is breaking down the barriers between Churches long separated, hostile or suspicious:

Gathering response as above.

Leader: Because Churches raised up, under God, by mission are now themselves sharing in mission beyond their own borders:

Gathering response as above.

Leader: Because He is revealing truths above Himself through the life and witness of Christians from other cultures:

Gathering response as above.

Leader: For the many ways in which Christians are reaching out in service to others:

Gathering response as above.

Leader: For the strong convictions of the young, and the vigour of their faith and witness:

Gathering response as above.

Leader: For the readiness of young people to serve others, at home or overseas:

Gathering response as above.

Leader: For the courage of those who face hardship, persecution or scorn in holding fast to Christ:

Gathering response as above.

Leader: For the demands of justice that will not be silenced and for all who strive for reconciliation between races, communities and nations:

Gathering response as above.

Leader: For every way in which God is everywhere at work:

Gathering response as above.

*It would be good if the Leader's lines were said by different people from all areas of the church and that they should be told to say the lines firm and true with a spirit of thanksgiving evident.

Praise

We praise You, God our father, for the wild riches of Your creation,
for the uniqueness of each person,
for the creativity, sustaining and renewing our cultures,
for Your faithfulness towards Your people.

ALL say twice: Praise be to You, O Lord.

We praise You, Jesus our Lord, for Your constant meddling in our affairs,
for Your identification with the poor,
for Your sacrifice for all men on the cross,
for revealing the true humanity to all people.

ALL say twice: Praise be to You, O Lord.

We praise You, God the Spirit, for Your inspiration of life,
for Your translation of the anguish of creation,
for Your insistence to draw us always to Christ,
for the infusion of unrest amongst humanity,
for the patient preparation of the fulfilment of history.

ALL say twice: Praise be to You, O Lord.

We praise You, blessed Trinity, for not doing to us according to our sins,
for continuing Your call to all that lives,
for continuing Your disturbing call to repentance,
for continuing life on earth

ALL say twice: Praise be to You, O Lord.

ALL SING verse three of 'Let us break bread' (beginning 'Let us praise God together') three times.

From WCC, Bangkok conference 1974, with additions

He does so much

Use a different voice for material that begins 'We praise you . . .'

Living God
we praise you
for your truth
which exceeds the grasp of our minds
but changes our lives.

We praise you
for your coming to us
in Christ
to make us your sons and daughters.

We praise you
for his coming and coming again
into our lives
so that your Word
is given utterance
even in our foolishness and weakness.

We praise you
for the promise
that broken hearts shall be mended,
that the poor shall hear good news,
that the imprisoned shall be liberated,
frightened people given confidence,
bad men made good,
and despair be transformed into hope.

Lord,
as we greet your coming of Christ
let us go with him on his way
through the world,
to share his suffering and his triumph,
until your purpose is complete
and all mankind rises in your image
glorious, free
and praising you for ever.

All things alive

Said by one or by the whole gathering.

O God,
You have called us out of death, we praise you!
　Send us back with the bread of life, we pray you!
You have turned us around, we praise you!
　Keep us faithful, we pray you!
You have begun a good work, we praise you!
　Complete your salvation in us, we pray you!
You have made us a chosen people, we praise you!
　Make us one with all people, we pray you!
You have taught us your law, we praise you!
　Change us by the Spirit's power, we pray you!
You have sent your Son in one place and time, we praise you!
　Be present in every time and place, we pray you!
Your Kingdom has come in His salvation, we praise you!
　Let it come always among us, we pray you! Amen.

Change is afoot

To stand before the Holy One of Eternity is to change.
To worship is to change.

We worship You Father in body, mind and spirit.
You want us to become whole people:
We would ask that we might worship You more completely.
Liberate and transform,
Touch our lives,
Let light permeate those areas we would hide,
Let light take away all darkness.
Praise to Your name,
Honour to Your name.
You have said,
Once you were in darkness,
Now you are in light:
The Light of the Lord.

How we honour and praise You,
How we thank and rejoice at Your name.

Based on some text found in One Heart, One Voice *by Andrew Maries (Hodder)*

God in all

God our Mother,
You hold our life within You,
Nourish us at Your breast,
And teach us to walk alone,
Help us to receive Your tenderness
And respond to Your challenge
That others may draw life from us.
Amen.

Without wishing to draw too fine a point, this prayer should not be seen as one that is best prayed by women. Obviously for saying by one person or the group as a whole.

Family

We are here
In the name of Jesus Christ.
We are sisters and brothers to him,
Daughters and sons of God.

To be said together, at the beginning of a service.

All to him

Female Leader: We have come to worship him, all to sing his
praise,
Joy or sorrow, grief or love, all to him we raise;
Praying in community, sharing hopes and
fears,
Giving time and energy, gladly gathered here,

> Laughing in our search of life, thanking God for love,
> In communion-fellowship, reaching high above.
>
> *Pause.*

Male Leader: One thing have we asked of the Lord, that we will seek:
To dwell in the house of the Lord
all the days of our lives, his beauty to behold,
to walk in his ways, to know him finally,
and sing his praise.

One half of gathering: His beauty to behold,
To walk in his ways,
To know him finally,
And sing his praise.

Other half to repeat.

Then all to say again the first section, 'We have come to worship . . . reaching high above'.

One with the Father

> With a clean heart I'll praise You,
> With a pure heart I'll honour You,
> With a right spirit within me,
> I will magnify Your name.
>
> Father make us one,
> That the world may see the Son,
> Release through us
> Streams of pure love,
> Father, make us one.
>
> Reign in me,
> Sovereign Lord, Reign in me.
> Captivate my heart,
> Let Your Kingdom come,

Establish there Your throne,
Let Your will be done.
Reign in me,
Sovereign Lord, reign in me.

Chris Bowater

Have these said by members of the gathering, where they are sitting.

Together with him

For the whole gathering to say.

We believe that where people are gathered together in love
    God is present
    and good things happen
    and life is full.

We believe that we are immersed in mystery
    that our lives are more than they seem
    that we belong to each other
    and to a universe of great creative energies
    whose source and destiny is God.

We believe that God is after us
    that he is calling to us
    from the depths of human life.

We believe that God has risked himself
    and become man in Jesus

In and with Jesus we believe that each of us
    is situated in the love of God
    and the pattern of our life
    will be the pattern of Jesus—
    through death to resurrection.

We believe that the Spirit of Peace
    is present with us, the Church
    as we gather to celebrate

our common existence
the resurrection of Jesus
and the fidelity of God.

And most deeply we believe that in our struggle to love
we incarnate God in the world.
And so aware of mystery and wonder
caught in friendship and laughter
we become speechless before the joy in our hearts
and celebrate the sacredness of life
in the Eucharist.

He confronts us

For all to say.

You are the beginning and the end of all life.
You captivate our hearts by your love.
You challenge our lives by your love.
You bring judgement upon us by your love.
You remove our fear by your love.
Let us with the whole of your creation live in your love
Now and always, in time and eternity.

Rex Chapman

Praise God

Choose different age-groupings to read the three 'We praise you' sections: a teenager, someone middle-aged, another elderly.

We praise you, God
for the world you have given us
for the life we have been born to
and the future that you promised us.

We praise you
for the liberty
the victory

and the new creation
Christ has won for us
by death and resurrection.

He has broken pride
and despair
and death
so that everything can be free
and new
and alive again.

We praise you
for his glory
higher than the skies
and brighter than the sun and moon and stars,
which penetrates
the darkest place of earth:
the hovel
and the slum
the place of hunger
and despair;
of sorrow
and loss
of greed
and lust
of loneliness and pain.

Always thanks

Voice:
Eternal God,
   we praise and adore you for everything you have done for
   us in Jesus Christ.
Voice 1: Because he lived as one of us and everything he did
   reflected your love,
Voice 2: Because he met the full force of the evil that drags us
   down but never gave in to it,

Voice 3: Because he lived his whole life in loving obedience
to you even though the road of obedience led to the
cross,

Voice 4: Because you brought him back from death to be the
Lord of the living and the dead, our thanksgiving will
never cease,

ALL: Our praise will never end.

He makes all things new

All: Yes: God our Father
                  sets our spirits free
                  when all the time
                       and everywhere
                       with silent thoughts
                  we are aware
                  that He is there
                       creating life in life
                       and love for life
                       in all the world
                       for me
                       and every struggling person!

Leader: So then we do not sit alone,
                       sweat alone,
                       sing alone,
                       fret alone.

All: We join with every being
                       everywhere,
                       every force
                       and every will
                       upon the earth
                       and in the air,
                       to hail our Lord,
                       to celebrate His day,
                       to laud and magnify,
                       to praise His glorious name.

A morning prayer of the Kingdom

ALL: We come to you, Lord. You, Lord, are opening our eyes. Give us your strength to speak of the wonder of your works.

Voice: You, Lord, are brightening the sky, stirring a new day;

ALL: Renew us with fire.

Voice: Because you, Father have given us back to your creation

ALL: We wish to be men and women of our times.

Voice: Because we seek to be more fully brothers and sisters in today's world.

ALL: We desire to hear and to realise the daily revolution which is fulfilling your creation.
We believe you made us and remake us with patience and affection.
We want to feel your firm, unseen hand;
that must bring fire,
that must bring struggle,
that must bring division,
that shall bring peace.

Voice: This is the day the Lord has made, let us be glad and sound his praise.

ALL: You, Lord make the morning sun to rise.
You speak many words to us through our brothers, sisters and our teachers, through our whole work and our whole life.
You give us from time to time a glimpse of who you are and what you are calling us to be.
You are the Father who loves us with passion,
You are the Son who is truth and life,
You are the Spirit who guides us to be true servants.

Voice: This Father has sent his Son, his strong Word, the complete expression of his love, to proclaim loud and clear the Kingdom of God, which is the fulfilment of our love and of all humanity.

ALL: Because we desire to be hearers of your word, and

    even more, doers of the word;
    bearing the full power of God,
    bearing the forgiveness of Jesus,
    bearing, for many, the proof and sign of God's love;
    we ask to hear again your trumpet of history that
    still sounds loud this morning.

Voice: To you be all the glory of the oncoming day through
    Christ, through our brothers and sisters in the bond of
    love, in the unity of the spirit.

ALL: Amen, amen, amen, amen, AMEN.

All honour to him

Leader: Jesus is Lord!

People: We belong to him!

Leader: All honour to you, Lord Jesus;
    you were taken and crucified by sinful men;
    you were forsaken by your friends,
    and you gave your life to bring all people to God.

People: We honour and praise your name!

Leader: All honour to you, Lord Jesus;
    God raised you to the heights
    and gave you the name above all names.

People: We acknowledge you as Lord
    and give praise to God our Father!

Leader: All honour to you, Lord Jesus,
    you have commissioned us
    to be your messengers.

People: As we honour you with our words and voices,
    help us to honour you with our lives.
    Amen.

The name above all names

Jesus, I worship you,
Worship, honour and adore your lovely name.
Jesus, I worship you,
Lord of Lords and King of Kings.

I worship you,
From a thankful heart, I sing,
I worship you.

Chris Bowater

This can be said by a number of people from different areas of the gathering and then followed by an appropriate song of praise.

Precious claims

Jesus has said very clearly:
    I am the love to be loved
    I am the life to be lived
    I am the joy to be shared
    I am the bread to be eaten
    I am the blood to be drunk
    I am the truth to be told
    I am the light to be lit
    I am the peace to be given.

Jesus is everything.

Mother Teresa

Choose eight people of differing jobs or none. Let each say their name and job. Then each says, 'Jesus has said very clearly' and then reads the line which follows from the last.

Always alive

Though we may be sad
lonely
bewildered
or afraid,
this is our time for celebration,
our time for telling each other
how good life is,
how full of possibility;

our time to greet love
and accept life;
our time to forgive
and be forgiven.

Lord,
we come to celebrate
Christ's dying and rising;
to look at life through his
resurrection eyes;
to greet your love
and to receive your life;
to ask forgiveness
and to forgive;
to sap the foundations of despair
and to go forward in hope.

Lord,
as we greet again
the coming of Christ,
let us go with him on his way
through the world
to share his suffering and his triumph,
until your purpose is complete
and all mankind rises in your image,
glorious, free
and praising you for ever.

Let all the gathering say the first statement. The first 'Lord . . .' can be said by half the gathering, the next by the other part of the congregation. The final four lines might be said by all with gusto and with no hesitant space left between 'until your purpose is complete' and 'and all mankind rises in your image'.

To encounter the Living God

Lord Jesus Christ
Living One,
dead once,
alive for ever,
we praise you
that, though we must die
death cannot keep us
because you want us.

You want us
to come to the Living God
alive with you,
alive with new life,
alive beyond life,
with knowledge beyond knowledge,
proud beyond the farthest conception of pride,
living where life was never dreamed of,
like a blaze of flame,
leaping high,
or a man lost in the dark
bursting into sunlight.

Lord
we step out to meet you
wherever you wish us to go:
we are afraid and puzzled
and sometimes hurt,
but fear will pass,
we shall see clearly,
our hurt will be healed:
thanks to you, Lord,
thanks to you.

This can be read across a row of people, each person having one line.

The Lord of life

Voice 1: Since Jesus Christ, out of love for this world,
gives his life, we can affirm
All: Love risks life!
Voice 2: Since the Holy Spirit incites us to love,
we can affirm
All: Love becomes action.
Voice 3: Our God is a living God.
All: Before time was, God lives.
Voice 3: He created the world and all living things.
All: He made us and sustains us.
Voice 2: In Jesus Christ he has drawn near to us.
All: He is with us always, even to the end of the world.
Voice 1: For us he died and rose again.
All: Death is swallowed up in victory.
We praise you, O God,
We acknowledge that you are the Lord of life.

So marvellous

Faith is weak
Life is hard
but Christ has died
and Christ is risen;
your Holy Spirit
is at work among us,
accomplishing more than we have ever thought to ask,
making us better men and women
than we ever thought to be,
making the world a brighter and more joyful place
than we could ever have imagined.

Lord, we praise you:
you are leading us to life's summit
and giving us the exhilaration of victory
over ourselves
over sin and death;

victory for ourselves
and all humankind.

Lord,
we worship and admire you;
we honour and adore you,
here and everywhere,
now and for ever.

Someone can read the first verse. The second might be read by non-teenagers, the last by those nineteen and under; or reverse.

Thank You

For surprises, especially on dull days
for smiles . . . they don't cost anything but
  they're worth their weight in gold
for people I get on with
for jokes . . . the kind ones!
for people who love me, even when I don't deserve it!
for colour, for contrast
for beauty of design and form
for animals who share our lives
for the sense of touch, and the rough, smooth texture of
  things
for raindrops on the petals of flowers
for sensitive people, who see more clearly than I do
for the clear, cool air of moorlands and hills
for love and the way it enriches life
for strength and a healthy body
for children . . . especially babies
for music . . . and music . . . and music
for the line of washing dancing in the breeze
for rain
for the sense of smell, especially Sunday lunchtime
for laughter and the way it charms you away from a bad
  mood
for warmth, especially on a winter day

for the ability to sense You . . . and to enjoy Your Presence
for home
for work to do
for everything that tests me . . . and shows what I'm made of
for incentives
for those scientists who choose to make our world interesting
   but do not spend their time devising methods of destruction
for creative minds
for books and reading
for the sense of taste, especially at Christmas
for birthdays
for small things that bring pleasure and the ability to enjoy
   them
for art
for friendship, that survives all sorts of things
for worship
for a sense of Eternity
for poetry
for choice . . . even when it's difficult

*At the end of this 'Thank You', the gathering might stand and say
together the Lord's Prayer, then lift hands high in the air at the point
when the words 'Thy Kingdom come' are said, and remain so until the
end.*

The Spirit directs

Father, Creator, Eternal Lord of all,
You make me in your image
You call me by name
You bring me back to myself and to you
I have sinned before heaven and before you.
I am sorry . . . I ask forgiveness.

Jesus Christ, Friend, Liberator,
Atonement of all.
You remake me in your likeness,
You come to me where I am

You heal my whole human life.
What have I done for you?
What am I doing for you?
What shall I do for you?

Holy Spirit, gentle presence,
Healing wind,
Love of God alive in man,
You heal our memories,
You send us to serve your world,
You lead us to the fulness of your family life.
Dwell in us, discern in us,
Direct us to our world's true needs . . .

William Hewett SJ

For three readers. Take a pause between each section. Ask people to think and meditate upon the words heard. Give the gathering time for reflection.

Power of the Spirit

Leader: Let us rejoice in the power of the Holy Spirit and give thanks.
Gathering: Let us rejoice in the power of the Holy Spirit and give thanks.
Leader: Let us rejoice . . .
Gathering: Let us rejoice . . .
All: Let us rejoice in the power of the Holy Spirit.

All sing: 'Spirit of the Living God, fall afresh on me . . .'

Leader: We recall the Spirit of God in the wonderful work of
        creation;
        we recall the work of the Spirit in the life of Christ;
        we recall the coming of the Spirit on the day of
        Pentecost;
        we believe in the renewing power of the Spirit today.

Gathering: Let us rejoice in the power of the Holy Spirit and give thanks.

Leader: We rejoice in the renewing power of the Spirit today.

*See end note.

Leader: Let us admit our reticence to be possessed and guided by the Spirit.

**See end note.

Leader: Let us pray for the power of the Holy Spirit in our relationship with God, in our sphere of living, with our nearest and with neighbours and friends, those at work, in our church, in the churches and gatherings everywhere, in our land and elsewhere;

Gathering: We rejoice in the power of the Holy Spirit. Send forth your Spirit, Lord.

All Sing: 'Spirit of the Living Lord, fall afresh on me . . .'

*We suggest direct testimony from members of the congregation can be given; or four speakers can outline a particular example that may be culled from a Christian journal, etc.

**In this second instance the same process can operate with particular individuals illustrating from the life of their church or broader (Christian) community, or bringing specific cases of this reticence as seen in the wider Church.

Adapted by Tony Jasper from material of which the original source is unknown.

The Holy Spirit

Come Holy Spirit
From heaven shine forth with your glorious light!

All: Come . . .
Come, Father of the poor, generous Spirit;
Come, light of our hearts!

All: From heaven . . .

Perfect Comforter! Wonderful Refreshment!
You make peace to dwell in our soul.
In our labour, you offer rest;
in temptation, strength;
and in our sadness, consolation.

All: From heaven . . .

Most kindly, warming Light! Enter the inmost depth of
    our hearts, for we are faithful to you.
Without your presence, we have nothing worthy,
    nothing pure.

All: From heaven . . .

Wash away our sin, send rain upon our dry ground,
heal our wounded souls.
With fire thaw our rigidity,
kindle our apathy
and direct our wandering feet.

All: From heaven . . .

On all who put their trust in you, and receive you in
    faith,
shower all your gifts.
Grant that they may grow in you, and persevere to the
    end; give them lasting joy! Alleluia.

All: Come, Holy Spirit, from heaven.

The Spirit comes as It wills

Come Holy Spirit, come just as You will,
Softly and gently as breezes so still.
Come as a rushing wind, mighty in power,
Come Holy Spirit, come now.

Come Holy Spirit, as flames from the fire,
Cleanse me, empower me, my being inspire.
Come as the healing oil liberally poured,
Come Holy Spirit, come now.

Come as a torrent, as waves on the sea,
Sweeping away all that would hinder me.
Come as refreshment, as streams from the hills,
Come Holy Spirit, come now.

Come Holy Spirit, come just as You will,
Work in and through me, Your purpose fulfil.
Make me much more like my Saviour, I pray,
Come Holy Spirit, come now.

Cause me to live as a child of the King,
One from whom worship and praise freely spring,
Bring Holy Spirit revival to me,
Come Holy Spirit, come now.

Chris Bowater

Have this said by different groupings within the church: e.g. one verse by elders (or whatever name), another by teachers and workers in the youth departments, etc.

The all-embracing Spirit

Holy Spirit, Creator,
at the beginning you hovered over the waters;
you breathe life into all creatures;
without you every living creature dies and returns to
    nothingness,

All: Come into us, Holy Spirit.

Holy Spirit, Comforter,
by you we were born again as children of God;
you make us living temples of your presence;
you pray within us prayers too deep for words,

All: Come into us, Holy Spirit.

Holy Spirit, Lord and Giver of Life,
you are light, you bring us light;
you are goodness and the source of all goodness,

All: Come into us, Holy Spirit.

Holy Spirit, Breath of life,
you sanctify and breathe life into the whole body of the
    Church;
you dwell in each one of its members,
and will one day give new life to our mortal bodies,

All: Come into us, Holy Spirit.

The Holy Spirit

Send forth your Spirit, Lord,
    Renew the face of the earth.
Creator Spirit, come,
    Inflame our waiting hearts.
Your spirit fills the world,
    And knows our every word.

Glory to God our Father,
    To Jesus Christ, the Son,
To you, O Holy Spirit,
    Now and evermore.
You are, you were, you come.
    Eternal, living God!

From Praise, *prayers from Taize*

Said by the leader or by all.

The Spirit like fire

Leader: It was the day of Pentecost:
the friends of Jesus were all together
in the house where they were staying.
Then it happened!

People: Suddenly, as if a storm of wind and fire
burst upon them,
they were filled with God's own power.
God gave them power to speak out boldly.

Leader: Lord, your Spirit is still coming
to give us power to change the world.

People: Come, Holy Spirit,
fill the hearts of your people
and set them alight with the fire of your love.

Leader: Lord, your Spirit is coming
to put your love into our hearts.

People: Come, Holy Spirit,
we will welcome you.
We will not be afraid.
Fill the hearts of your people
and set them alight with the fire of your love.

Seeking the Kingdom: Introduction

'Upside-down'

Riddles and puzzles beg to be asked—and human nature loves to solve them. That's why thousands of people every day religiously complete a crossword and why hours of life are given over to 'adult toys' like the Rubik's Cube. One puzzle, however, which is not for solving is what is described in the Bible as the Mystery of the Kingdom of God. We are warned not to try and solve it because we cannot define and circumscribe the Kingdom of God any more than we can contain or limit God to time and space. It is a mental impossibility, just as going through the eye of a needle or standing on one's head for any length of time is a physical impossibility.

We can nevertheless learn a great deal about the Kingdom from Jesus's teaching and particularly his parables. These parables can help us, not to solve the mystery of eternity, but to begin to sort out the muddles in our thinking and living.

One of the clearest challenges in Jesus's teaching on the Kingdom is the way 'God's Rule' turns upside-down our sense of what is right and wrong, just and unjust.

To read: Matthew 20:1–16, 'The Riddle of the Workers in the Vineyard'.

Jesus said, 'The Kingdom of God is like this story—those who enter into God's society at the last minute are given as big a welcome as those who come early.' In human terms fairness is about everybody getting what they deserve—a good wage for a good day's work. In God's terms, however, fairness is about everybody getting what they need. God's generosity knows no limits in making this possible.

To reflect: Note down ways in which the following passages challenge your values:

'The Kingdom of God as a new community' (p. 83).
'Listen to the outcast within you' (p. 58).
'Masculine and feminine' (p. 75).
'A fool's prayer' (p. 67).

The Kingdom of God

The Kingdom People—an African perspective.

1. In the Kingdom people listen to each other and share with each other.
2. The Kingdom is not merely future but begins here and now (without the here and now being an end in itself).
3. The Kingdom is made up of individuals who, without denying their individuality, are also a community as 'the people of God'. The 'extended family' is a useful model for understanding this. Also the 'returnees' from Nigeria were absorbed into their families and communities. There are no refugee camps in the Kingdom of God. Also those who have gone before and those who are to come are part of the community of the here and now, and this is a sign of the Kingdom.
4. The Kingdom opens our eyes to the evils that beset us— especially racism and tribalism. We need to be purged of these as part of realising our full humanity and membership of God's Kingdom.
5. The Kingdom deals with the realities of life.
6. The organising principle of the Kingdom is love.
7. In the Kingdom there is worship and joy and prayer for each other—and all this is 'mission-orientated'. A sign of the Kingdom people is that they know how to live in a global community. They are no longer limited by their own localities.
8. Being in the Kingdom enables us and allows us to do more together—it is a work place, a place where we 'build each other up'.

9. In the Kingdom the Holy Spirit is the facilitator and it is *everyone* who is enabled to make his (or her) contribution.
10. We don't need to 'speak and think the same'; with all our variety, conflicts, differences of view, we can still know a unity and inter-relatedness that, again, are signs of being in the Kingdom of God.

Christian celebration

Christian celebration as I understand it is knowing that the Kingdom of God is present now and becomes present in the lived moment. It involves offering the creation and agony in this day to a God who transforms and makes things new. It is entering and knowing that each of us is into the creating and redeeming which is now making humankind. Christians are people, a people, with a destiny, with memories, with expectancies. They know there is a song to be sung, a journey to be made, a territory to be claimed.

Tony Jasper, based on thoughts by Ross Snyder

Human Needs

Welcome

This can preface a hymn or prayer.

Jesus spoke often about 'The Kingdom of God': a kingdom
very different to the kingdoms of this world; a kingdom with
very different values and priorities—ones which challenge
many of our assumptions about life.

In fact, it has been said that 'to begin to understand the
gospel of Jesus Christ, one must first learn to stand on one's
head!' (G. K. Chesterton)

Corrymeela Community

See the Kingdom

See the kingdom he is building,
Share the new world he reveals,
See him walking there, see him smiling here
On rich and poor, black and white, young and old, you and me.

Hear the words he speaks, hear the call he makes,
Share the good news he reveals.
Hear him talking there, hear him laughing here
With sick and well, east and west, good and bad, you and me.

Sense the hope he brings, sense the trust he shows,
Share the kindness he reveals;
Sense the person there, sense his presence here
To grow and spread, raise the dead, conquer lies, forever
rise, forever rise.

William Hewett SJ, Care Of Living Streams

Have this said by a mixed bunch of people.

Not as we are

Said by all

Great God, we come to you with all the marks of sin upon
us, with our anxiety and doubt, our sickness and our
spiritual poverty.

We come with all the weakness we have not the strength to
change, with unfulfilled longings and awareness of things
we will never achieve.

We come, asking you to help us believe that your grace is all
we need, that your power can come to its full strength in
our weakness; that in spite of all that we are not, you can
take what we are and give expression to your life-
renewing love.

We come in the name of Jesus, to rediscover ourselves in the
rushing, cleansing, healing force of his resurrection, and
to rise with him, confident and strong, honouring and
serving you in this world and in eternity.

Lord help us

L: Lord, the solitude and isolation of others frightens us,
because it mirrors our own solitude and isolation. We
feel cut off from the successful and talented, the wealthy
and popular, the strong and the carefree. We find it is so
difficult to step outside the polite phrases, the empty
smiles and the conventional behaviour, and
communicate authentically with each other.

R: Lord, help us.

L: We are afraid that others will not accept us because we
do not fully accept ourselves.

We use loaded words which are an evasion of truth rather
than an expression of thought.

We are willing to hurt those who hurt us.

We are too easily impressed by money, titles, and the
outward signs of success.

R: Lord, pardon us.

L: Make us ready to understand and appreciate the hopes, fears, and struggles of others, so that in the creative encounter of friends we may discover a new quality of life. Give us grace to take time for relationships without agendas or time-limits, and occasionally to sink into the silences where the spirit may reflect on the deep and true things of life.

R: Lord, renew us.

L: We remember the loneliness of the neglected wife, or nagged husband, the loneliness of the widow and widower, the loneliness of the boy at boarding-school or the child in an orphanage, the loneliness of the cripple or the mentally ill, the loneliness of the deserted wife, the divorced husband, and the illegitimate children.

R: Lord, lead us.

L: Teach us to be kind to those who seem vulgar, naive, or ungifted; to be patient even when we are in a hurry, to see the point of wise regulations even when they inconvenience us, and to create that community of love which is the ultimate antidote to our private loneliness.

R: Lord, hear us, for your Kingdom's sake. Amen.

Finding his true reflection

It would surely be good
if now and then we could look into Paradise
and meet God like a friend
under the trees in the evening air.

Then we could discuss
this or that with him
in a friendly atmosphere.
We could tell him the news from the world,
what he should change
so that we could really be pleased with it.

All history,
not just the history of the Cross,

but that too, and that above all
stops my dictating to God
what he should do.

So my prayer takes the form of pain
at the fact that my heart, my home and my city
do not reflect the splendour of existence,
the ground and source of which is God.

These are things, God, of which you alone are Lord.
These you bestow, I know,
with boundless and incomprehensible generosity.
The greatest of them is love,
hope's sister, the companion on our way.
If I open my eye
You can remove the plank from it.

But beyond that,
you have left the organisation of the world to us.
There is no point in repeating;
O God, give, remember, do—
We are the ones who have to give, do and remember
and then say: we are worthless servants.
Here is our body and the work of our hands,
brittle, bitty, unfinished.
Through them we tried to express
something that defies all expression and to which
you are calling us.

Halina Bortnowska

Use one voice.

Father forgive them, for they know not what they do

By praying with the guilty and condemned,
    with Jesus on the cross:
    for all facing trial or in prison,
    and all captives of sin:
Bring them to look up to his holy cross:
    and, hand in hand with him, go free.

By praying for the present help of thine own Spirit,
    that all thou givest me to do
    may be fearlessly begun,
    and faithfully finished.

So help me God to pray with Jesus on the cross
    and to commend my body, mind and spirit,
    O Father, into thy hand,
    for life, for death, for time without end.

Eric Milner-White

Use one person, but suggest to the gathering that this may be their prayer. Read fairly slowly so that people have time to digest what may be their thoughts and sentiments.

Listening to God

Standing with Him

To be said by the whole gathering.

God
our mother, our father,
when we pray, teach us to realise that we are
inextricably bound up with the answer.
May we cease crying like a child,
may we realise that when we pray we do so
standing within your recreating purpose.
Teach us that real intercession is not merely a petition, but
it involves perfect, costly self-surrender to You.
Lead us to affirm our desire to serve You.

God
our mother and father,
you call us to be grown men and women,
responsible for life and lives.
It is only when we stand with You and your recreating
purposes,
in desire and intention,
that we can think of the needs of the Church, and the world
in your name.

Tony Jasper: based on words by J. Neville Ward, The Use of
Praying *(Epworth).*

He is all

God of compassion, in mercy befriend us;
Giver of grace for our needs all-availing,
Wisdom and strength for each day do Thou send us,
Patience untiring and courage unfailing.

When you started off the universe

When you started off the universe, Lord most high,
did you know just what would happen as years went by?
Did you in your infinite mind
everything foresee?
Or does being God mean you make a place for uncertainty?

When your Son allowed himself to be led away,
did he know you'd resurrect him on Easter Day?
Could he, there on Calvary's hill,
know what was to be?
Or did being yours mean he had to suffer uncertainty?

When we're told our faith has got to be more assured,
does it mean we ought to know all the answers, Lord?
If we had true faith in God,
would our doubts all flee?
Or does having faith mean we thank you Lord, for
   uncertainty?

John Gregory

*This, as with many extracts, lends itself to being said by a number of
voices. Here, rather than changing the voice with each verse, someone
different could read each question.*

I know the spirit

Said by one person.

I know the spirit in this mortal frame
Marked with personality and name
Can, by awareness, any given hour
Ally itself with God. Then all the power
That floods the Universe with living light
Can surge and flow through me, and lift my sight
To higher levels, hushed and glad and free,
Until I know that God is touching me.
But like a child with book or game or ball
The span of my attention is so small!

Louise Sullivan

Living with uncertainty

For one voice.

Uncertainty, surprise and shock
belong to life.
Religion is often seen as deliverance
from uncertainty—
but would a totally certain life
be a human life,
worth living?

Brian Wren

God of listening

Read by one person, with everyone saying the first verse after all verses have been read.

God of listening, God of peace,
In our hearts may you increase,
Till our flow of words shall cease,
And we hear you.

Listening is the hardest skill,
Silences we strain to fill,
Far too restless to be still
And just hear you.

If our well-planned words defeat
Words of others that we meet,
Hesitant and incomplete,
Father, hear them.

If the insights that we seek
Come from someone tired and weak,
Looking for a chance to speak,
Help us hear them.

(Verse 1 may be repeated here.)

Janet Shepperson

To Him

Our Person Up There,
May Your name give you street cred.
May Your Kingdom become pretty radical.
Do anything You want to
down here as well as Up There.
Give us some nosh where we need it.

Forgive me for beating up the people who You forgive for
          doing something to me in the first place.
                    Don't let Judgement Day arrive
                 and keep us safe from Baddies.

                              Amen

                                                    Paul Wilson

His will be done

          God, lover of us all,
          most holy one,
          help us to respond to you
          to create what you want for us here
          on earth.
          Give us today enough for our needs;
          forgive our weak and deliberate offences,
          just as we must forgive others
          when they hurt us.
          Help us to resist evil
          and to do what is good;
          for we are yours,
          endowed with your power
          to make our world whole.

                                                Lala Winkley

For saying as a gathering.

The rice you eat

     Remember, when you eat this rice
     You eat my sweat,
     You too were born a man or woman.
     This rice, this daily pleasure
        to the rich and to the poor—
     Behind it stands my bitter pain.

The stalks are pushed up by my shoulder's strength,
A long time passes between sweat and seed,
The ripened gold is packed with work.
How many drops of sweat are held in each?
I grow your rice, my tendons stretch to breaking,
I sweat red clay,
I pour my strength into the ground,
The rice is my seed.
It is my body and my blood,
Eat it! Do you find it—good?

Modern Thai folk song

Have one person to read as far as 'my tendons stretch to breaking'.
Then another.

Awareness to . . .

Listen . . .
to the outcast within you . . .
the only one whence healing and reconciliation come . . .
the only one who can bring salvation to the part of you
that speaks loudest and thinks strongest . . .

In your inscape, as well as in the landscape of the wider
    world, the voice of the poor and the oppressed has priority
    over the voice of the dominant . . .
We must not refuse to become aware of all that we find
    distressing or painful or fearful within: if we do, we shall
    merely project onto others our inner darkness . . .

Are you white and afraid of your blackness? . . .
Are you male and afraid of the feminine within? . . .
Are you heterosexual and afraid of your homosexual feelings?
Are you rich and afraid of your poverty? . . .
Are you young and afraid of being old?
Are you healthy and afraid of your mortality?
Are you able and afraid of disability? . . .

Are you busily involved and afraid of being useless? . . .
Nothing is to be expelled as foreign . . .
All is to be befriended and transformed . . .

Be in love with life,
wrestle with chaos and the pain,
with your self and with others,
spirit echoing Spirit,
trusting in the victory of the vulnerable,
glimpsing the peace,
the wholeness,
the justice
and the joy
that comes from following the Pioneer
made perfect in suffering,
striving and yearning and crying out
from the very depths and heights
of the world's anguish and the world's bliss,
and so becoming friends and partners of God
in the divine creating . . .

June Cotter

This needs to be taken fairly crisply, otherwise it could become somewhat 'earnest' and 'religious' and so lose its sting. It might be said by a group, with the middle questions said separately.

Our need

Heal us, Immanuel, hear our prayer,
We wait to feel thy touch.
Deep wounded souls Thee repair,
And, Saviour, we are such.

Martin Broadbent

Together, or by an individual for all.

The stone tomb

Leave to one very good reader.

This sudden still
Forces the black cross
Towards us each,
Dark culprits
At the face of all.

This man is now
Washed from our leets,
Escaped our jeers,
Darker wears
Things from the dreaded truth.

There was ghostliness
In what we did
That I reflect on
When ghostlier
Thoughts return to me.

All's for the stone tomb
Where we encased
Bitter reflections,
Watching faith
In case it should rise on us
Wearing his hands.

Gerald Kells

The pillar of salt speaks

But Lot's wife
behind him
looked back,
and she became
a pillar of salt
(Genesis 19:26)

Why did I look back?

I was afraid of the two strangers
Who came to our home last evening.
They said, 'we' were good,
But 'they', our neighbours, were bad.
Lot was so pleased
That he did a big *namasthe* to them
And asked me to prepare a feast.
Lot said they were angels.
But I was afraid of them.
Their faces were cold, their looks harsh,
And their eyes burning with anger.

Why did I look back?

I was angry at Lot.
When the men surrounded our house
And wanted the strangers to come out,
Lot offered to send our virgin daughters to them.
Both the girls were engaged to be married.
I was angry. Very angry. Outraged.
I pushed them into the little store.
I stood guard against it.
Over my dead body.
When those men wanted men
Why send girls to them?
Why didn't Lot himself go?
Why didn't the two angels go?
That would have been an angelic happening.

Why did I look back?

Because my neighbours were out there.
When, during the birth of my first child
I cried out in pain,
The women were there.
They held my hands, wiped my brow,
Gave me water to drink.

And when the baby was born
They bathed it and put it to my breast.

> And where was Lot?
> He was out in the fields
> Praying to his God.

When my little girl hit her foot against a stone
And broke her toe nail,
My neighbour came with some crushed leaves
And put them round her toe.
My daughter smiled through her tears.

> And where was Lot?
> He was out in the fields
> Praying to his God.

You say only the women were good
But the men were bad?
When there was no water for three days,
And my children were crying,
My neighbour's husband walked three miles
To get water. And he gave us some.

Why did I look back?

Because I wanted to perish with my neighbours
Rather than be saved without them.

Stanley J. Samartha

For the right words

Sometimes I think I do not know how to properly pray—
except in church.
There the words are dressed in rich robes:
the syntax folded precisely into place,
the hook of order
matched exactly to the eye,
and overall
the embroidery of inflection and tone.

Left on my own—
in the house, on the street, at my desk—
the words jump up and down
in clumsy nakedness,
in the middle of
crying children, barking dogs, washbaskets,
roaring motors, crowded rooms, TV commercials,
dancing teen-agers, committee resolutions,
school buses, empty rooms, grocery stores,
doctors' offices, kitchen sinks, traffic jams,
computer labs, reception rooms, trash cans.
Lord of my life,
I cannot depend on grammar,
punctuation and sentence structure.
I can depend on You.

It's me, it's me it's me, O Lord,
standing in the need of prayer.

Anne Springsteen, from It's Me, O Lord

Involve the gathering. Have three people stand centrally. One reads as far as 'left on my own'. Each reads one of the next thoughts. Then all three from 'the words' to 'the middle of'. Now have members of the gathering come out and read each of the following thoughts, particularly if they reflect them: e.g. traffic jam by a traffic warden, motor patrol policeman, etc. All to read form 'Lord of my life' and, if the whole gathering has the words, then all the last two lines.

The true peace

O God, author of peace and victor over death, we give you thanks that from the beginning you have gathered a people to be the instrument of your reconciliation, never leaving your world untended. Grant unto all your servants that peace which the world cannot give, that our hearts may be

set to carry on the work of peacemaking and that we may
abide in the love of Jesus Christ our Lord.
Amen.

Sojourners Fellowship, Washington DC, USA

One voice.

Fit

When

I was a child
I understood
like a child

thought
like a child

spoke
like a child
broke
like a child

Yet

now I'm a man
I am not fit
for the Kingdom of God

Now I'm supposed to be a man
I've put away the Plan for Man
I've put away my childish things
my child-like things
and most of my feelings

Suppressed them all like the sinner I am
lock them up like only man can

Look in the mirror
Forget what I am

A man without faith
and a double-binded man

And so

I'm not fit
for the Kingdom of God

*A different male voice could read the sections: 'When . . . child'; 'Yet
. . . man can'; and both read the remainder.*

Those who shall lead

Confession

Eternal God: in every age you have raised up men and
women to live and die in faith. Forgive our lukewarm lives.
You have commanded us to speak; we have been silent. You
have called us to do your truth; we have been fearful. Have
mercy on us, your weak, reluctant servants. Keep in mind
faithful people for us to follow, so that living with courage
and love, we may inherit the kingdom promised in Jesus
Christ, and reign with him forever. Amen.

For the gathering as a whole.

He is with us

Leader: The Lord be with you,
         with you and within you,
         with you in your pious fears,
         with you in your twisted doubt,
         with you as you worship,
            as you dream and dance and shout.
         May the Lord get through to you!

All: And to your spirit too!

Come to Him

Leader: Come to Him for He is light.
All: No darkness shall cover us.
Leader: Come to Him for He is truth.
All: No falsehood shall deceive us.
Leader: Come to Him for He is love.
All: No hate will destroy us.
Leader: Come as you are and He will make you what you will be.
All: We shall be renewed by Him.
Leader: Come to Him for he is the door.
All: By Him if we enter in we shall be saved.
Leader: Come unto Him.
All: And we shall find rest.

Clifford Johnson

God of Surprises

All day in his presence

We are sons of the morning;
　　We are daughters of the day.
The One who has loved us
　　Has brightened our way.
The Lord of all kindness
　　Has called us to be
A light for his people
　　To set their hearts free.

*From the hymn 'City of God' by Dan Shutte; and here we see it said at
the beginning of worship by the leader or the general gathering.*

A fool's prayer

Father and God of Fools,
　　Lord of Clowns and Smiling Saints,
　　I rejoice in this playful prayer
　　that You are a God of laughter and of tears.
Blessed are You, for You have rooted within me
　　the gifts of humor, lightheartedness and mirth.
With jokes and comedy, You cause my heart to sing
　　as laughter is made to flow out of me.

I am grateful that Your Son, Jesus,
　　who was this world's master of wit,
　　daily invites me to be a fool for Your sake,
　　to embrace the madness
　　of Your prophets, holy people and saints.

I delight in that holy madness
    which becomes the very medicine
    to heal the chaos of the cosmos
    since it calls each of us
    out of the humdrumness of daily life
    into joy, adventure,
    and, most of all, into freedom.

I, who am so easily tempted to barter my freedom
    for tiny speckles of honor and power,
    am filled with gratitude that Your Son's very life
    has reminded me to value only love,
    the communion with other persons and with You,
    and to balance honor with humor.

With circus bands and organ grinders,
    with fools, clowns, court-jesters and comics,
    with high-spirited angels and saints,
    I too join the fun and foolishness of life,
    so that Your holy laughter
    may ring out to the edges of the universe.

Blessed are You, Lord my God,
    who invites me to be a holy fool.

Amen.

Edward Hays

Use different voices for the 'I' statements.

Hot faith

God, but I want madness!
I want to tremble, to be shaken,
to yield to pulsation,
to surrender to the rhythm of music and sea,
to the seasons of ebb and flow,
to the tidal surge of love.

I am tired of being
hard,
tight,
controlled,
tensed against the invasion of novelty,
armed against tenderness, afraid of softness.
I am tired of directing my world,
making,
doing,
shaping.

Sam Keen

This needs passion and energy, yet should be read with restraint; for the sentiments are for all, and not as some might think, especially if read 'over the top' for the very way-out.

His address is everywhere

Dear God,
may your Spirit live in us.
May the hot wind of the northern desert,
the cold wind from the South Pole,
the fresh breeze from the Pacific
bring us the power of your Spirit.
Help us to deepen the inner life
of our churches, in Chile* and Britain*:
make us one in your Spirit.
Help us to follow the ways of peace,
cherishing forgiveness and reconciliation.
Help us to be the voice of the poor
and powerless, who cannot express,
their huge needs and hidden hurt.
Help us to work for change,
with those who are oppressed.
Help us to do the work
of the ancient prophets in today's world.
We trust in your power, God,

but help us also to work hard.
We thank you for making us part
of your people, a network of caring covering the world.
Amen.

Alicia Gutierrez, Chile

* *Leave or change, as desired.*

Said by all.

O God I am chained

O God I am chained
to my images—

       Daughter, Sister, Tomboy,
       Brain, Sweetheart, Housewife,
       Mother, Chauffeur,
       Cook, Hostess.

Am I all of these? Torn?
Disintegrated?
Or none?
No, I cannot deny them.
They have become part of me.
But somewhere
Slipping silently between
         the images,
Is there someone else?
Someone whole?—
       Poet? Pastor? Mystic?
       Scholar? Music Maker?
       Counsellor? Lover? Friend?

How shall I know?

And you, God,
are you also chained and hidden

by your images, your names, your roles?—
    Creator, Judge, Father, Redeemer, King, Saviour,
    Christ, Son of God, Holy Spirit, Light . . .

Are you also lost among the images,
struggling to emerge into new roles,
fresh revelations of your real self?

Are you not also
    Poet?   Becoming?
     Artist?   Suffering?
      Mother? Loving?
       Daughter? Changing?
        Mystery? Singing?
          Rejoicing?
          Darkness?
          Despair?

Can we emerge together, you and I?
Can we break the chains that bind us
  and move out into the fresh air of liberation?

Call me into being, God!
And let me catch a glimpse of you as you really are
  in this moment of time and eternity!

Betsy Fisher Phillips

*This could be said by a variety of women using, e.g., a different voice
on daughter, sister, etc. and accordingly on other lists.*

Conference poem

    I, wearing my badge of identity,
      unique, God-given,
    put labels on my neighbour
    and write off her opinion—

'Oh yes—she would say that,
  being Jewish
  or middle class.'

'Oh yes—that's what I'd expect to hear
  from Marxists
  or evangelicals.'

'Well, you know, that point of view
  is typically charismatic.'

I
have my deeply felt convictions.
The rest ride hobby horses,
  perversely, with baffling words
  or clichés.

Lord, how hard it is
to hear, and hear, and really understand,
to see, and see,
and turn for healing.

Use another voice to express the 'points of view'.

Walking on water

Walking on water is difficult,
  but I have seen it done.

Those with enough grief to sink them
  have kept on—
drawn by an invisible source of strength:
  they were not let down.

Crossing this sea some swim
  and many drown—
  a few there are
  walking on water.

Cecily Taylor

Use one voice.

God and man and woman

This can be read by two people standing apart, allowing for pauses for thought as appropriate.

A: In the beginning, God made man.
He was so disappointed that he tried again.
And the next time, he made woman.

B: EVE, THE FIRST WOMAN, WAS A VEGETARIAN.
SHE LIKED APPLES, AND ATE THE WRONG ONE.
MEN HAVE BEEN SUSPICIOUS OF VEGETARIANS EVER SINCE.

A: Noah didn't eat apples.
He was a man . . . so he drank alcohol.
In fact, he drank so much alcohol that one day
    his sons found their old man completely sozzled
    and lying in the nude.
Women have been suspicious of alcohol ever since.

B: LOT DIDN'T EAT APPLES OR DRINK WINE.
HE JUST LIVED IN A CITY WHERE THE MEN DIDN'T KNOW
    WHO THEY FANCIED.
SO GOD TOLD HIM TO LEAVE THE CITY, AND SO HE DID.
GOD SAID, 'DON'T LOOK BACK, FOR I'M GOING TO BURN
    DOWN THE CITY.'
SO LOT DIDN'T LOOK BACK, BUT HIS WIFE DID
AND SHE WAS TURNED INTO A PILLAR OF SALT.
WOMEN HAVE NEVER LOOKED BACK SINCE.

A: Delilah didn't eat apples, drink wine or look back.
She was a hairdresser.
Samson didn't know that,
    but while he was resting his macho muscles,
    Delilah cut his hair and took his strength away.
Men have avoided being bald ever since.

B: St Paul didn't know Eve, Noah, Lot or Delilah.
But he did know some women,
 and those he did must have given him bad
  memories.
Because he told them not to speak in church,
 not to go into a church without a hat,
 and always obey their husbands.
Paul also said that men should not get married
 unless they were unable to control themselves.
Men have been unable to control themselves ever
 since.

A: But Jesus was different.
He was strong, but he cried.
He even cried in front of other men.
He knew that some women had bad reputations,
 but that didn't keep him back from them:
He knelt beside them.
He loved his disciples who were all men
 and he wasn't afraid to tell them that he loved them.
And though he was never married,
 he was always surrounded by women who, at his death,
 were more faithful to him than the men.

Jesus didn't make a fuss about who was who, or what
 was what.
He said that everyone who loved him was his mother,
          his sister,
          his brother.

B: Thank God for Jesus.

Iona Community

Gender superfluous

Masculine and feminine
I would not use
when I speak of God
in creation, in saving,
in coming, in dying,
in rising, in forever living,
for God speaks to all
humankind, humanity, humans.
My Jesus did not die
to make better masculines
to make better feminines
He died to make us all
whoever, whatever
whole.

Tony Jasper

Two readers together, or separately as wished: female to read word 'masculine' and male to read word 'feminine', on both occasions.

Knocking

A: Knock and it shall be opened unto you.
B: Behold I stand at the door and knock.
A: Knocking, knocking,
B: there is always someone knocking,
A: if you listen you can hear them.
B: Sometimes the knock is a very timid one,
A: soft,
B: apologetic.
A: Knock, knock.
B: I'm terribly sorry to interrupt, it says,
A: I hope I'm not disturbing you,
B: I know I haven't an appointment . . .
A: You're very important and I'm very insignificant,
B: I almost hope you won't hear me.

A: Knock, knock.
B: Oh yes, thank you, here I come,
A: so sorry to trouble you,
B: I know you're a very busy man.

A: Sometimes the knock is perfunctory,
B: a mere formality,
A: knock knock,
B: and walk straight in,
A: don't wait for anyone to say 'come in'
B: because you weren't really asking permission to enter,
A: just going through a little routine,
B: a mere formality,
A: knock knock,
B: and walk straight in.

A: Sometimes the knock is a sort of signal,
B: an understood sign between friends,
A: knock knock-a knock knock, knock knock.
B: Here I am, it says, it's me.
A: Oh, it's you. Well don't stand knocking. Come right in.
B: Thanks. Here I am.
A: Knock knock-a knock knock, knock knock.
B: Ah! there's Bill. I know his knock. Come right in.
A: And sometimes the knock is very loud,
B: proud,
A: arrogant,
B: imperious,
A: knock, knock, knock,
B: hurry up there!
A: Open this door!
B: Keeping me waiting!
A: Don't you know who I am?
B: Come on, come on!
A: Knock, knock, knock.
B: Ah! and about time too.

A: And sometimes the knock is quite different,
B: quiet

A: but not timid,
B: gentle
A: but not afraid.
B: Behold I stand at the door and knock . . .
A: courteous
B: but not a mere formality,
A: waiting
B: but not impatient,
A: firm
B: but not aggressive,
A: a sort of signal
B: but not many seem to recognise it.
A: But those who do recognise it, open the door
B: and he comes in
A: and they eat together
B: and what a meal!
A: Happy are those who open the door.

B: And what about those who do not open?
A: He still stands there knocking . . . knocking . . .

John Horner

Unfortunately some of the text failed to make its rightful appearance in At All Times And In All Places. *Hence, the full text here.*

Creative living

Take one moment of my life, Lord,
one fractured, frenzied moment,
when I have bullied the children
or quarrelled with my friend,
re-opening the wounds of history
and gloating over unforgotten bruises
like a miser over gold;
or when I have watched the news,
raged wildly at the brutal, ugly mess of the world's pain,
only to change channels and forget it;

or when I have given my all in meetings, speaking
grand ideas and ecstatic visions,
only to be too tired and cross to play with the baby.

Take one moment of my life, Lord,
one of those moments,
for these are the ones I am afraid to show you—
the times when I am selfish and unreliable,
unreasonable and proud,
when I get fed up with loving,
bored with being good,
sick to death of hearing about God,
and I don't care whether or not I pray.

It is at times like these that I need you,
Jesus Emmanuel,
God with us,
God with me,
God who joins me in the sordid complexities of life,
the subtle webs of compromise,
the strain of mislaid good intentions,
the weariness of choice,
the cloying, sticky sweetness of temptation.

The God who joins me—
not to batter me or burn me with your judgement,
however righteous, however true—
but to love me as I am, the unlovely,
to comfort me with tears in your eyes.
At moments like these, I need to know that you love me,
even though I hate myself.
At moments like these, I need to know
that you know what life is like.
For it is those tears, that pain in the heart of God,
which give me the honesty to see myself,
as I am, as I can be,
and with the seeing,
the strength and will to be renewed.

So take one moment of my life, Lord,
onto your Cross.
Draw it into the dark fire of your love,
so that, broken,
healed,
transfigured,
cleansed,
reborn,
it may be lived,
even yet,
in praise.

Julie Hulme

Use one voice or a number of voices on 'It is at times . . . sweetness of temptation' on the third and the final stanza.

Mingled in all our living

Mingled in all our living, your presence, Lord, I feel,
Closer than my own sighing, your love sustaining me,
You cause the pulse of blood, Lord, to flow in every vein,
My heart responds in gladness, life's rhythm beats within.
    O Lord of earth and heaven, I give my life to you,
    Loving you in my neighbour, praising you in the world.

You stand beside the worker in factory and farm;
daily, incessant clamour sounding a hymn of life,
In every hammer's pounding, typewriter's clacking key,
We hear a tune of praising creation's melody,

You're in the sound of laughter and in the flow of tears,
sharing with all your people the fight for human good,
You came in Christ incarnate that life might be redeemed,
pledging us to your kingdom, helping the world to change.

Mortimer Arias

Words and tune of this song can be found in Gentle Angry People.
Although intended for singing we think the words can be used for prayer/meditation.

Someday soon people will . . .

Someday soon people will celebrate life every day.
But we would like to do it right now,
wet and wild and risen with our Lord.
Someday soon people will send up balloons in church.
Turn tired old cathedrals into cafeterias.
Paint gravestones as bright as the sun.
Know that they are beautiful, black red or white.
Glimpse the face of God in their patient parents.
Use the eyes of friends in place of mirrors.
Bounce through the mountains on beachballs.
Write their Christian names in the sunset.
Become as free as that man called Jesus the Christ.
Sink their teeth into politics for peace.
Turn all bombs into boomerangs.
All bullets into blanks.
Slow down and listen to the Universe.
Slow down and wait for God.
Baptise their babies with love before birth.
Celebrate Easter as angels do below,
And hang Christmas banners on the moon.
Yes someday soon people will live like that,
but we plan to start right now.
Right now Lord. Right now.
Amen, Lord, right now.

Norman Habel

*Read as a gathering, fairly fast. Although this has a late 1960s ring
(indeed, that is the time of its writing) it still possesses that
'something'.*

Lord, teach us to face our fears

Lord,
teach us to face our fears
may we understand the dangers that threaten us
enable us to receive those things of which we are afraid and
to befriend them
you tell us not to be afraid
in Jesus you have overcome all the powers of evil and
destruction
you can turn the evil that we have done, the evil done to us,
around
you can make all things good, the very way in which we can
find new life
you are the God of surprises.

Tony Jasper, based on words found in God of Surprises *by Gerard
W. Hughes (Darton, Longman & Todd).*

One voice.

Be whole

Voice 1:
God is love
There is no room for fear in love
We love because God loved us first.

Voice 2:
It takes courage to look steadily at ourselves and still to love
ourselves . . .

Silence.

All:
God, loving and accepting,
we are afraid of your love, your intimacy.
We are used to being judged,

but we are not used to being loved,
totally.
We would rather hold on to our self-hatred
than believe in your total acceptance of us.

Give us the courage to let you and embrace you;
may we learn how to want you to touch us, to know us,
that we in turn may love generously
those who cannot believe they are loved.

Silence.

Let go . . .
Let be . . .
Let God . . .

*Each turns to their neighbour and offers a sign of acceptance and love,
saying: Brother and Sister, be healed, be whole.*

God in Community

The Kingdom as a new community

Love-hate,
joy-sorrow;
birth-death
work-leisure;
all the action
and the inter-action
of human life
in quickly changed patterns,
like sunlight on tossed water,
held together
in its depths
by culture
kinship
dignity.

What if culture is invaded,
kinship severed,
dignity destroyed?
What if the depths no longer hold
the whirling shapes
in balance?
What if hatred, sorrow, death
and endless leisure
make one unbroken shadow?
Can community be restored?
Can the sunlight dance again?

There was a man
who was all light,
who pierced the shadow

and plumbed the depths;
who created
new ties of kinship,
gave value to each culture
and to each human life
new dignity.

There is a God
who holds all things together.
In Him
there is
a new community.

Betty Hares

Use a different voice for the questions, from 'What if culture is invaded' to the end of 'Can the sunlight dance again?'

Lord you have brought us together

Leader: Lord, you have brought us together from all of our different backgrounds to share this time at Corrymeela with each other. Make us open to you and to each person here.

All: OPEN OUR EARS

Leader: To hear what you are saying to us in the things that happen and in the people we meet.

All: OPEN OUR HANDS

Leader: To reach out to one another in friendship and to help when help is needed.

All: OPEN OUR LIPS

Leader: To share our stories with one another and to bring comfort, inspiration, joy and laughter to each other.

All: OPEN OUR MINDS

Leader: To discover new truth about you, about ourselves, about each other and about our world.

All: OPEN OUR HEARTS

Leader: To welcome one another freely—just as you welcome us.

All: THROUGH JESUS CHRIST. AMEN.

Corrymeela Community

Strings, wires, rapes and chains

Sometimes they are called
Bill collectors
And other times they are called
Friends.

Sometimes they are called
Obligations
And at other times they are called
Relatives.

Sometimes they are called
Burdens
And other times they are called
Sons and daughters.

Sometimes they are called
A lot of different things
And other times they are called
The choices I have made.

Together we are
Bound
Inexorably
On our very own
Constructive/destructive
Road(s) to
Jerusalem(s).

Conrad Weiser, Dancing All The Dances. Singing all the Songs

Different voices can be used for the various 'Sometimes . . .' stanzas, with all saying the last stanza.

Prayers of confession

God, you created us to live in fellowship with you and with one another.

Forgive us for thinking we can love you without showing love for others.

Open our eyes to see the whole of your family—neighbours in need and far away.

Open our hands to share generously the gifts you have given us in life.

Call us back from our failures to love in the past and free us for service in the future,

through Jesus Christ our Lord.

AMEN

For one or five voices; if the latter, then obviously each to take a sentence.

Who said we are different from . . .

L: Here we are, O Lord, comfortable and secure, remote from

    —the people who don't fit the mould . . .

    —the tensions of society . . .

    —the demands of home and family . . .

    —the joys and crises of our daily work . . .

R: Lord, call us.

L: Here we are, O Lord, conscious that we are

    —weak and hesitant to trust your way . . .

    —obstinate and headstrong with our own plans . . .

    —clumsy and insensitive to the needs of others . . .

    —guilty of nursed resentments, ugly thoughts, and unkind reminiscences.

R: Lord, forgive us.

L: Here we are, O Lord, engaging in public prayer and private thought, aware that we need

    —a richer quality of life . . .

    —a deeper sense of peace . . .

    —a new experience of freedom . . .
    —a wider vision of service . . .

R: Lord, touch us.

L: Here we are, O Lord, remote from
    —the homeless refugee and the persecuted minority . . .
    —the wayward rebel and the lonely aged . . .
    —the hardened criminal and the forgotten pervert . . .
    —the harassed mother and the alcoholic father . . .
    —the hurt, the sad, the foolish, and the desperate in our society.

R: Lord, challenge us.

L: Here we are, O Lord, ready to serve as well as reflect, ready to face the truth about ourselves as well as the truth about others, ready to open our hearts and share our resources, ready to lift our prayer from the level of a cultic act to the realm of authentic action.

R: Lord, accept us, for your Love's Sake. Amen.

There you will find Him

Ch: Where love is, God is.

R1: I saw Him in a loving relationship between two people.

R2: I saw Him when a man shook hands with his brother after a quarrel.

R3: I saw Him when a couple offered a home to an ageing parent.

Ch: Where patience is, God is.

R1: I saw Him when a woman listened to a bedridden neighbour who had no-one to talk to.

R2: I saw Him when a mother spoke gently to her child after a tantrum.

R3: I saw Him in the exercises of the man who had suffered a stroke.

Ch: Where health is, God is.

R1: I saw Him in the men and women healed in our hospitals.

R2: I saw Him in the joyful leaping of healthy children.

Ch: Where suffering is, God is.

R1: I saw Him in the anxiety of the mentally ill.

R2: I saw Him in the faces of the parents whose child had died of leukemia.

Ch: Where communication is, God is.

R1: I saw Him in the honest discussion of parents and a teenage child.

R2: I saw Him when a man spoke to another about his faith.

Ch: Where employment is, God is.

R1: I saw Him in prison sewing mailbags.

R2: I saw Him in the efforts of an employer to retain his older staff.

R3: I saw Him in the hiring of a discharged mental patient.

Ch: Where beauty is, God is.

R1: I saw Him with the coming of the bud in springtime.

R2: I saw Him in the stained glass window of a cathedral.

Ch: Where self-giving is, God is.

R1: I saw Him in the unpaid helpers at a school for the handicapped.

R2: I saw Him in voluntary social workers.

R3: I saw Him in the pastor caring for his people.

Ch: Where action is, God is.

R1: I saw Him in the world-wide response to a disaster appeal.

R2: I saw Him in the service of the church in many countries.

R3: I saw Him in the action of a congregation which spent as much on others as it did on itself.

The upside-down Kingdom

Leader: What does it mean to be blessed?
The world often thinks it means to be wealthy, hold power, never experience any difficulty, get things your own way—have life easy. But listen to what Jesus says:

Reader 1: Blessed are you poor, for yours is the Kingdom of God.

Reader 2: Blessed are you who mourn, for you shall be comforted.

Reader 1: Blessed are those with a gentle spirit, for they shall have the whole earth as their inheritance.

Reader 2: Blessed are those who hunger and thirst for righteousness, for they shall be satisfied.

Reader 1: Blessed are the merciful, for they shall obtain mercy.

Reader 2: Blessed are the pure in heart, for they shall see God.

Reader 1: Blessed are the peacemakers, for they shall be called children of God.

Reader 2: Blessed are those who are persecuted in the cause of right, for the kingdom of heaven is theirs.

(Matthew 5:3–10)

Leader: These sayings of Jesus which we call the 'Beatitudes' run counter to all the world holds out as producing 'happiness'. They announce a 'blessedness' based on embracing poverty, mourning, peacemaking, and even persecution. Jesus invites us to enter God's Kingdom by allowing our lives to be turned upside-down, with the promise that if we do so, we will find ourselves—perhaps for the first time— actually living 'right-side up'.

Corrymeela Community

Saturday night and Sunday morning

Dazzling lights veiled in smoke
attended by the serpent beat
a herd of legs and swinging hair
bewitches the hour

He sits and drinks and taps his foot
long into the disco groove
and flashing lights bombard his mind
in mesmerising mood

Ashtrays crammed with headless tabs
impatient to be removed,
a broken glass, a silly laugh
stave off the cold, cold dawn

Pews, bare and stark
sprinkled with spinsters,
he stands to sing the opening hymn
of everlasting love.

Martin Eggleton

Ulster stills

Letters, thrown like dice from Holy Writ
fall noiselessly down—
games played by budding Theologians
jostling for obscurities.

Blood, sprinkled on the ground
betrays a hidden gun—
snaps in black and white
taken for tourists.

Clichés, bound in gold-leafed awe
fly from pulpit steps—
loud-mouthed pastors
goading on their sheep.

Beer, laced with boredom, awaits a youth
tattooed in bigotry—
absorbing the Irish jokes
within the froth.

Slogans, daubed in sectarian paint
adorn the crumbling walls—
software for soldiers
in armoured tanks.

Martin Eggleton

For one voice.

Office hours

My swivel chair
Is the pivot of the office world:
Whirling in a small confine
Of daily duty—
A service to mankind, they say—
Biscuits, mere trifles,
Entertainment
Or heavier metals,
Each as important
As the rhythm of the seasons;
God's symphony:
Or so they say—
But how?
Paper, aged with lines of ink,
Never growing free
The sap of life
Lopped in its infancy—
Telephones for flirting,
Little breakers foaming
Into a dull sea-scape
Of stark statistics:
Struggling with print
And the smell of photocopying ink—
The wholeness
Of this crisp new parchment,
A gift box of eight fresh hours,
Pierced and punctuated

Wearing thin the fabric
Of a polite facade—
A pale and ghostly courtesy
Through whose ever-thinning veil
We must perceive
The truth—that the
Endless
Pages of print
Can never disguise.

J. R. Brooke

For one voice.

Lord of all worlds

Lord of all worlds that are, Saviour of our world: redeem
your whole creation. Order unruly powers, deal with
injustice, feed and satisfy the longing peoples, so that in
freedom your children may enjoy the earth you have made,
and cheerfully sing your praises, through Jesus Christ our
Lord. Amen.

For one voice.

A litany of intercession

For the reconciliation of mankind through the revolution of
   non-violent love: WE CALL ON THE SPIRIT
For the established churches that they may be humbled,
   reformed, and united:
For the global movement of peace and liberation, the church
   of Jesus incognito:
For all poor and hungry, migrant workers and hobos,
   outcast and unemployed:
For the people of the streets and ghettos, for children
   unwanted in their homes:

For the wounded, for prisoners and exiles, all those
    persecuted for conscience or resistance:
For victims of discrimination, harassment and brutality:
For the sick and suffering in mind and body, for those
    freaked out on drugs or fear:
For all oppressors, exploiters and imperialists, that they may
    be confused and disarmed by love:
For the masters of war, N.N. and N., that they may be
    given a new transplant in place of their heart of stone:
For uptight authorities, police and officials, especially N. and
    N., that they may all listen to the voice of the humble and
    meek:
For all whom we fear, resent, or cannot love; for the unlovable:
For the liberation of our twisted lives, for the opening of closed
    doors:
For those who ar dying and have died, whether in bitterness or
    tranquillity:
For doctors, nurses, and social workers, for ministers to the
    poor:
For organisers, students and writers, all who raise the cry for
    justice:
For all who are close to use, here and in every place:
That all couples may realise their union with the universal
    flow of love:
That our tables may be spread with the natural fruits of the
    earth:
That our grandchildren may inherit a restored planet:
That we may have desire to study the books of ancient wisdom:
That people's revolution everywhere may become humanised
    and democratic:
That each one who enters our house may receive the
    hospitality due the Christ whom he bears:
That with compassion and fidelity we may work for renewal
    to our life's end:
In thanksgiving for all who have turned away from exploitation,
    especially N:
In thanksgiving for all who have been freed from the prisons
    of this world, especially N: WE CALL ON THE SPIRIT

Here the leader shall ask for free intercession from the people. When they are finished, the Deacon shall conclude:

We call on the Spirit to bind us in solidarity with all who are
   using their lives to resist evil and affirm community:
   WE CALL ON THE SPIRIT

From A Covenant of Peace: A Liberation Prayer Book.

The phrase 'We call on the spirit' might be used more often. Different voices can say the various lines. Obviously there can be an extension of some thoughts and some might wish to specify victims, exploiters, etc.

Go in peace, go in love

Go in peace, go in love,
   finding joy in each other.
Go in peace, go in love,
In Christ we're sister and brother.
Led by his Spirit there's strength each day,
   Light for the way together.
Go in peace, go in love,
May God be with us for ever.

Corrymeela Community

For all.

The Kingdom is Within You: Introduction

'Inside-out'

Jesus taught that the tax collector who could not find the words to pray was nearer the kingdom of God than the pharisee whose prayers were endless. So also the woman who washed Jesus's feet with her tears understood Jesus and his role better than Simon who'd laid on a lavish meal. Through these comments and many more, it is clear that the people we honour are not necessarily the same as those whom God honours. The people who are put down and pushed out are the ones he lifts up for everyone to see. In them we are invited to see the Glory of God.

To read: Luke 7:36–50 (compare the account in Luke with Matthew 26:6–13 and Mark 14:3–9).

If you're reading those passages in a group it may help in discussion to divide into three smaller groups, Group 1 to take the role of Simon, Group 2 the woman and Group 3 the disciples. After discussion in small groups your feelings and hopes as that character return to the larger group and, still in the role, share together how you see the situation.

Note how in Matthew and Mark the woman is not described as sinful. Somewhere, apparently, in the telling and re-telling of this story her reputation has been scarred.

Note also how in spite of Jesus's words that 'everywhere the Gospel is preached her name will be remembered' the fact is her name is *not* remembered—indeed her name has not even been recorded. Like so many women and marginalised groups history has written this woman out of the script, losing the details that give her importance and profile.

To reflect: Which characters/situations in the following poems tell you most about yourself? What sort of people do you admire? How do you feel people see you?

Dying in the street (p. 126).
Yo Ella—I am she (p. 113).
I can speak with some knowledge (p. 132).

Spirituality

He is holy

Creator:
Holy is your being
At your hand is your ruling,
Done is your desiring.

Our bread provide us,
Our debt forgive us,
From trials free us.

Liturgy of the People's Church, Berkeley, California.

To be said by all.

The hardest thing

I'm not very good at being holy,
but in spite of me,
You've called me to heal
in Your name.

I asked you for power to do your will.
You said I didn't need it.

Only—
to love you a lot.

Beth Webb

One person, at an appropriate moment.

Lovers of all

Tender God, touch us.
Be touched by us;
make us lovers of humanity,
compassionate friends of all creation,
Gracious God, hear us unto speech;
speak us into action;
and through us, recreate the world.

Amen.

Carter Heyward

To be said by all.

For wholeness

O God,
Giver of Life
Bearer of Pain
Maker of Love,
you are able to accept in us what we cannot even acknowledge;
you are able to name in us what we cannot bear to speak of;
you are able to hold in your memory
what we have tried to forget;
you are able to hold out to us the glory
that we cannot conceive of.
Reconcile us through your cross to
all that we have rejected in our selves,
that we may find no part of your
creation to be alien or strange to us,
and that we ourselves may be made
whole.

Through Jesus Christ, our lover and our friend.

Amen.

Have the leader or someone read the first four lines, then all to read the remaining.

In his way

Living Christ,
you suffered for us,
we offer you our own suffering—

the physical pain
that weakens us;
the pain of loss and loneliness;
the pain of failure
that undermines our confidence;
the pain we bring on ourselves through selfishness;
the pain of broken relationships,
unkind thoughts,
cruel words,
insensitive actions.

We offer you our suffering
so that you can teach us patience
and courage
so that what is destructive
can become creative
and make us whole human beings again.

We offer our suffering to you
and we accept yours,
as we see it in the sorrow of our neighbours,
in the grief of those who mourn,
the anguish
of those who get no relief from pain,
the deep distress
of those whose children
have been suddenly killed,
or have died the lingering painful death
of hunger;
the misery of those who are forgotten
and ignored;
society's misfits
and inadequates.

We accept your sorrow in these
and we take up our cross,
to sacrifice ourselves on the altar
of humanity's needs.

Lord,
make our suffering true;
make it the suffering of those who hunger
and thirst for what is right
and just,
and true;
make it the suffering of those
who know
that they have never done enough
until no one suffers any more.

Keep us from self-pity and from whining;
undergird our pain
with the joy of hope
which is deeper than sorrow and stronger
than death
and with the love
which cannot be taken away from us.

Let us see at last,
your full resurrection glory
which puts an end to sorrow, crying, pain
and death,
for ever;
then our praise
will be perfect and endless
and you will receive
the honour that is your due.

*Have a different group of people, whether by church office/job, career,
task or occupation to read the various 'We offer . . .'*

Walking rightly

Excuse me God,
but religion doesn't agree with me.
When I pray and hold you precious
every minute of every hour,
going to Church twice every Sunday,
doing the right thing,
saying the right thing—
although I do it with all my heart,
it wears me out.

Dragging my life up to you,
I grow weird and weary.
I straddle two worlds
and succeed in neither.

Please God,
if it's alright with you,
may I just walk calmly,
common-or-gardenly,
not-very-holily—
grateful for your hand,
which does not always burn,
but always heals.

Sometimes we may meet in a
flash of lightning,
but mostly—
may I praise you in a smile?

Beth Webb

One person.

Physical contact

'Touch Me' You say,
'Heal Me for I am tired and heavy laden,
comfort Me for I am weary and hard pressed.'

—I touch all I see in Your name Lord,
I do all I can—

'Touch Me' You say
'For I am lonely, and I weep alone,
stay awake and sit with Me.'

—I hold all I see in Your name Lord,
I weep all I can—

'Touch Me' You say,
'Like Magdala, with your hair, your eyes,
your arms, your hands.
When you pray, touch Me
with your whole self,
and I will be comforted.'

Beth Webb

One person.

Killing time

I'd used to want to change the world—
I still do—but I came to see
the world was changing on its own
and also changing me

So I believed!—in apathy
I'd used to think I'm killing time
but then I came to see
time passes away all on its own
and was also killing me

I said my God what have I done
to reap such vanity
And He replied not very much
that's one of the traits of apathy

I retorted that's not fair
but then again selfishness never is
And he should know as it's been reported
His Son's murder warrant was sealed with a kiss.

And I had thought I'd only killed time
that only the world would have to change
but when I saw who made them both
my concepts were soon rearranged

Time doesn't come back from the dead
nor does a soul that's bound in sin
I was engaged but not yet wed
to a system that was planning on being my coffin

But in desperation I found life
and now I've come to see
I'm in but I'm not of this world
and only God is changing me.

Use various readers for the 'I's' or, have one person to read.

Somebody for . . .

Mary held You baby-safe
wrapped in holy mother-care

May those of us who've known no love
Find a little comfort there.

Beth Webb

One person. For a mother with newly born child perhaps? She could

then take and show her baby to the gathering and all could give thanks
for new life. Or the man could do the same, or, yes, both together!

The pearl

Lord,
show me who you are
by seeing you
where you are;
help me
in my search for truth,
not just to draw
the bounds of right and wrong,
the edge of heresies
but to find you
beyond the line
alien to me.

Teach your Church, Lord
to learn,
to learn from other learners,
to feel the peace
that others find
by naming other names,
to see the light
outside the walls
as reflections of the
light within.

Help me, Lord,
sifting through the net,
to find new pearls
and one that holds me
in its beauty,
until I learn the secret
of grace

and let the other
take it from my hand.

Martin Eggleton

Use one voice.

Human Dignity

Saint Patrick's breastplate

Christ be with me, Christ before me,
Christ behind me, Christ in me,
Christ beneath me, Christ above me,
Christ on my right, Christ on my left,
Christ where I lie, Christ where I sit,
Christ where I arise,
Christ in the heart of every man who thinks of me,
Christ in the mouth of every man who speaks of me,
Christ in every eye that sees me,
Christ in every ear that hears me.

May your salvation Lord, be ever with us.

AMEN

One row to say line 1, then as they say line 2 the next row says line 1 and so on. Eventually all to say together.

Poverty is my cross

Poverty is my cross
my colour binds me to it.
Charity offices the stations
on the road to Golgotha.

Goaded by the creditors
I drink the tears I weep.
Bills of credit
the spear drawing blood.

Strung on my cross
I suffer the agony of poverty.
Goddam them!
They know what they've done.

James Matthews, Cry Rage

One voice.

Stay with him

Lord
I'm angry.
Angry at all I see around me,
the violated places,
signs of the insignificance
of property, open spaces,
and people,
people's faces,
violated by apathy,
daubed with indifference,
sprayed without meaning.
Lord, give me anger
which is righteous
or else the anger
adds to the violence.

Lord,
I'm not sure that I believe
as others do,
they seem so sure, as if
the words were chiselled in their brain
to fill their mouths with truth
as firm as rocks.
But I can only tread
as if the road ahead might
not take the measure of my doubting;
yet you walk with me

so I can believe
then the way is worth my walking.

Martin Eggleton

For one voice or spoken by a small mixed group.

Seek the truth

Seek the truth
　　Listen to the truth
Love the truth
　　Serve the truth
Teach the truth
　　Live the truth
Defend the truth
　　Unto death.

Johan Devananden, Sri Lankan Workers' Mass

One voice.

If I should kiss you

If I should kiss you
as Christ now does,
would I mean it and would I dare?
Could I embrace and talk you through
the turmoil of your fading days?
Would my caress be a sullied stroke
or a hand of hope?
In all the phone numbers
you pursued, entertained, seduced and loved,
did you find the right man?
The one empty of deceit,
compassionate, celibate and complete.
Communion, for you, was always
the predictable business of bodies.

And men who choose women
are afraid to touch men who don't
but I would now like to hold your hand
because of a man
that I'm in love with.
The one empty of deceit,
compassionate, celibate and complete.
With him there is no grave
only laughter.

Stewart Henderson

One voice.

Dignity and Sexuality

AIDS . . .

God,
You are true love,
You created us in your own image,
You gave us sexual drives.
Under your guidance we would seek to know the positive
    meaning of discipline and control.
Enable us to deepen our most treasured relationships
Take us away from the misuse of the body's creative powers
May we learn personal and social wholeness.

God,
we pray
for women and men who for one reason or another suffer
    illnesses that have a sexual derivation.
In your presence, in theirs, may we offer love.
Remove from us thoughts of condemnation and rejection.
Teach us to listen and to hear the cries of those who suffer.
Root out from us negative feelings and deep-rooted fears.

God,
we pray
for all agencies, doctors and nurses,
for all like them who will give care and understanding.

God,
we pray most for those who suffer.
What words, what thoughts of ours, Father, are sufficient?
At very least lead them from this darkness to your most
    marvellous light.

Tony Jasper

One voice, or different people for each verse.

Last night I saw

Last night I saw a hawthorn tree.
I knew it would bud soon—
And yet there was no sign,
Nothing to show,
Just an ordinary bare branch.

Then I wondered
How many people I knew
Were like that twig?
Seemingly bare and barren,
Showing no promise,
Who would suddenly
Burst into life
And beauty and strength
With me having
No hand in it whatsoever.

Ken Walsh, Sometimes I weep *(SCM)*

One voice.

My sister, my friend

I knew I would meet you
   my sister, my friend
Look in the mirror
   of your eyes and see
   the main of Managua
earthquake revolution
your son killed
your daughter crippled
   with polio
and as if that were not
   enough
four years ago your husband
disappeared with another woman,

'Triste' you say shaking your head.
'Things are worse now' you say
    water rationed
three pounds of rice for four each week
yet you left food on your plate, could
    not eat.
    Mother of the maid,
you wash clothes for others by hand
    in your only dress
    and clean for them, too.
A hard life of labor
    yet the smiles come through.
Church fills the gap
    suffering made in your heart.
Jesus walks in the fountain
    of your tears.
Why this suffering
natural and unnatural
    disaster yielding grief
    impaled in your heart?
I'm forty-seven and you are forty-six,
'She looks twenty years older than you',
I remember
the whistles men gave me
as we walked to the park.
No one gives you a second glance now
your brown body wrinkled and worn
    but your smile is shy
    and kind
    shines through the mirror
    I see you
    my sister and friend
        Nicaraguense.

Sarah Hornsby

One voice.

Yo so Ella—I am She

Listen to women. Listen to their yearning.
Listen to their anger. Try to understand,
Understand oppression,
Understand them without control
   over their bodies,
   over their labour,
   over their lives.
Together, understand, and move.

We have been robbed of our wisdom.
We were close to God, close to the earth.
Now we buy the goods of the earth in plastic
   wrappers.
We sit in cold pews to hear men talk of faith.
What of our experience of faith?
We have lost what was our own.
We must reclaim wisdom, reclaim power, reclaim ourselves.

I am She.
I have been robbed and raped.
A long time ago—I was Wisdom.
I knew about my body, my powers.
I knew from years with my children
   about the depths of human experience.
I have been burned at the stake.
Now I pay doctors and psychologists
   to tell me what my grandmothers knew.

From Things Hoped For: General Globe of Ministries,
United Methodist Church, USA.

*Suggest a group of men say the first verse and then women read the
remainder.*

Don't call me Mama

Don't call me Mama
Don't call me Mother,
See me for what I am
A Woman.

Even though you crawled
I pushed you out from under me.
I teased you with my breast.
It gave me pain
It gave me pleasure
It gave you life.

Don't call me Mama
A stalwart of the nation.
Don't call me Mother
The backbone of the struggle.
See me here for what I am
A Woman.

Throughout our history
You call me Mother
You ban your belly
And call me Mama.
How much longer?
Will you learn?
My Motherhood is not my Womanhood
Just another dimension
of me
A Woman.

I am here in the struggle
I am here—part of the nation
I am here in Afrika
I am here in Britain
I am here in the Caribbean
I am here in the Americas

I am here on the Frontline
A Woman.

Mama, Mother
A sign of respect.
When you call me Mama
Do you see my Woman?
When you struggle for sustenance
between my breasts,
Call me Mother, Tower of Strength,
Keeper of Tradition
Do you see my Woman?

Before my belly bloated with another life,
My teeth clenched
and the sweat of labour
burnt my eyes
I was Woman.
Before you called me
Before you whispered 'Mother'
Before you cried out 'Mama'
I was Woman.

When you mourn my passing
Mourn my Woman.
Don't call me Mama
Don't call me Mother
See me for what I am
A Woman

Carole Stewart, Watchers and Seekers

Use different voices an appropriate nationalities (if possible) on the stanza beginning 'I am here . . .' to its end. Use women only, and have all read the last four lines.

Woman's creed

I believe in God, who created woman and man, in God's own image,
who created the world and gave both sexes care of the earth.

I believe in Jesus, child of God, chosen of God, born of the woman Mary
who listened to women and liked them, who stayed in their homes,
who discussed the kingdom with them, who was followed and financed by women disciples.

I believe in Jesus, who discussed theology with a woman at a well,
and first confided in her his messiahship,
who motivated her to go and tell her great news to the city.

I believe in Jesus who received anointing from a woman at Simon's house,
who rebuked the men guests who scorned her.

I believe in Jesus who said this woman will be remembered for what she did—minister for Jesus.

I believe in Jesus who healed a woman on the sabbath and made her straight
because she was a human being.

I believe in Jesus who spoke of God as a woman seeking the lost coin, as
a woman who swept seeking the lost.

I believe in Jesus who thought of pregnancy and birth with reverence
not as a punishment—but as a wrenching event
a metaphor for transformation—born again—anguish into joy.

I believe in Jesus who spoke of himself as a mother hen
who would gather her chicks under her wing.

I believe in Jesus who appeared first to Mary Magdalene
who sent her with the burning message . . . GO AND
TELL.

I believe in the wholeness of the Saviour
in whom there is neither Jew nor Greek, slave nor free, male
nor female,
for we are all one in salvation.

I believe in the Holy Spirit as she moves over the waters of
creation and
over the earth.

I believe in the Holy Spirit the woman spirit of God,
who like a hen created us and gave us birth and covers us
with her wings.

Rachel C. Wahlberg, from No Longer Strangers

Different people on each verse.

Towards a community of women and men

Reader 1: For every woman who is tired of acting weak when
she is strong,
Reader 2:   there is a man who is tired of appearing strong
when he feels vulnerable.
Reader 1: For every woman who is tired of acting dumb,
Reader 2:   there is a man who is burdened with the constant
expectation of 'knowing everything'.
Reader 1: For every woman who is tired of being called an
'emotional female',
Reader 2:   there is a man who is denied the right to weep
and be gentle.

Reader 1: For every woman who is called unfeminine when she competes,

Reader 2:   there is a man for whom competition is the only way to prove his masculinity.

Reader 1: For every woman who is tired of being a sex object,

Reader 2:   there is a man who is tired of pretending to be a sex machine.

Reader 1: For every woman who feels 'tied down' by the children,

Reader 2:   there is a man who is denied the full pleasure of shared parenthood.

Reader 1: For every woman who is denied meaningful employment or equal pay,

Reader 2:   there is a man who must bear full (financial) responsibility for another human being.

Reader 1: For every woman who was not taught the intricacies of an automobile,

Reader 2:   there is a man who was not taught the satisfaction of cooking.

Reader 1: For every woman who takes a step towards her own liberation,

Reader 2:   there is a man who finds the way to freedom has been made a little easier.

Corrymeela Community

Lust—a protest

But, Lord—you're a Spirit:
Pure, unconfined, unshackled
Untrammelled—free
Lassitudes of lust
Dulling the spark of Divinity
Resident in mortal flesh
Have no place in your fire
For you don't allow them room;
Self control, your Spirit rules

Over unclouded vision
Mountain peak coldness
Almost freezing in its clarity
But not frozen—
The fires of your love
Oversee your truth
And melt it into the
Balm of your Breath—
And yet—
You came in human form
A frail body like mine
From dust to dust
But yours transformed
No sin to corrupt
Temptation trampled down
By the force of your yielded will
Wielding power of two-edged strength
Deadly sword thrusts, and no offspring
To rise again:
You were the one who arose—
Life out of broken, abandoned rights
And I am to be joined to you;
But still upon this earth
I live in a house of clay
Perishable, fragile, needing daily care
(And I know you keep a tally
Of the ebb and flow of my strength,
Every strand and coil accounted for)
But still the glory is also my bane
My shame taints the windows
With grime,
My soul sits enshrouded in gloom
Spirit crushed, subdued,
Save when I lay hold of you in faith:
Jesus, you love me and I
Am complete in you:
Whole, pure, radiant
The clay becomes burnished gold

Yet only for a moment—this day,
But it has been done, accomplished
Once and for all:
And the angels are moved at our
Privilege—
Lowly dust,
A firmly-trod foundation,
Humbly equal with the sky
As it is clothed
In the Son's righteousness:
And one day, I will understand:
Face to face.

J. R. Brooke

One person.

Heavy duty lace or sea poem

Placid expanse,
Spreading sight
As keen as eagle's eyes,
The eddies soothed
With tiny ripples,
Serenely rushing,
Smoothly stippling its surface—
Stretched over the roar
Of the cavernous echoing boom—
Hallowed by the hurl
Of the force of the wave's welling water,
Whooshing its strength,
Swirling the sway of its curve,
Curling the cream of the foam
Swooping like fish
Shoals of surf
Crashing in thunderous splashing,
Crushing the stones,
Pebble-dashing,

Breaking the thunder
Sundered in surges
By the clamour
Of rock-hewn, spewed spray
Strongly sucked
Swelling to small starred specks,
Trickles timidly moving
Forward flowing
Back into the blue, green-grey of the deep—
Mirrored by the moon
Moving over the vastness of the vault above,
The walls of the womb
Wavering reflections
Of what is hidden beneath.

J. R. Brooke

One person to read.

Knowing ourselves

A newborn child does not know
its own boundaries or identity.
Life means growing into self-awareness.
'I know that I am' and 'I know that I know'
are epoch making statements
from which flow thinking, reason
imagination, creativity.

Yet not all humans reach such self-awareness.
Some have only limited powers of thought
yet can still love and be loved.
Fulness, then,
is different from normality.

Louise Sullivan

One person or a couple with child.

Essential

I take my freedom
lest I die
for pride runs through my veins . . .
For I am he who
dares to say
I shall be Free, or dead
today . . .

Mari Evans

One voice

Present

This woman vomiting her
hunger over the world
this melancholy woman forgotten
before memory came
this yellow movement bursting forth like
coltrane's melodies all mouth
buttocks moving like palm trees,
this honeycoatedalabamianwoman
singing rhythm of blue/black/smiles
this yellow woman carrying beneath her breasts
pleasures without tongues
this woman whose body weaves
desertpattern,
this woman, wet with wandering
reviving the beauty of forests and winds
is telling you secrets
gather up your odors and listen
as she sings the mold from memory.

there is no place
for a soft/black/woman.
there is no smile green enough or

summertime words warm enough to allow my
growth.
and in my head
i see my history
standing like a shy child
and i chant lullabies
as i ride my past on horseback
tasting the thirst of yesterday tribes
hearing the ancient/black/woman
me, singing hay-hay-hay-hay-ya-ya-ya-
hay-hay-hay-hay-ya-ya-ya-
like a slow scent
beneath the sun
and i dance my
creation and my grandmothers gathering
from my bones like great wooden birds
spread their wings
while their long/legged/laughter
stretched the night
and i taste the
seasons of my birth. mangoes. papayas.
drink my woman/coconut/milks
stalk the ancient grandfathers
sipping on proud afternoons
walk like a song roung my waist
tremble like a new/born/child troubled
with new breaths
and my singing
becomes the only sound as a
blue/black/magical/woman. walking
womb ripe. walking. loud with mornings. walking.
making pilgrimage to herself. walking

Sonia Sanchez

Have read by someone who feels and knows how to read words.

The miracle

Before you were conceived
  I wanted you
Before you were born
  I loved you
Before you were an hour
  I would die for you
This is the miracle of life.
The pain, so great,
was more than the throbbing of your final journey
into my love
But part of a process
that came accompanied with
New Life
New Consciousness
New Understanding
New Wisdom
A bigger heart
To accommodate
New Love
At last Liberation
At last Freedom
How special, how valuable
How close to all things right
Nine months of worry and expectation
Brought more than imagination can conjure
Never really knew
Until . . .
I feel you coming
I am ready for you
I am ready for life
I am rejuvenated
I am Blessed
with the gift of life.

Maureen Hawkins

From Watchers and Seekers: Creative writing by Black Women in Britain, *edited by Rhonda Cobham and Merle Collins (The Women's Press, 1987).*

To be said by one woman who is expecting child.

If a child . . .

If	If
a child lives with criticism	a child lives with encouragement
she learns to condemn.	he learns confidence.
If	If
a child lives with hostility	a child lives with praise
he learns to fight.	she learns to appreciate.
If	If
a child lives with ridicule	a child lives with fairness
she learns to be shy.	he learns justice.
If	If
a child lives with shame	a child lives with security
he learns to feel guilty.	she learns to have faith.
If	If
a child lives with tolerance	a child lives with approval
she learns to be patient.	he learns to like himself.

If
a child lives with acceptance and friendship
he or she learns to find love in the world.

Julius Nyerere, President of Tanzania, Speech to Royal Commonwealth Society.

Have two groups facing each other; one says the left hand column, the other, the right.

Dying in the street

Megga
  your child dying in the street!

  We ran to my brother
  not yet sixteen
  The men with guns
  stood at his side
Megga
  hugged him
  rocked him
  tried to kiss life back
  into those still lips
  saw the desperation
  still mirrored in eyes
  which would not close
Megga
  held her head
  her wail was a cry of the centuries
  rising and clawing the highest
  pinnacles of anguish then ebbing
  away to mere grief only to be picked up
  in some other womb
  Only to reverberate in the bosom of
  some other woman who sees her reflection
  long and clear on a blade
  random and merciless
  The halter to strangle the instincts
  Your child dying in the streets!
Megga
  knows I stand firm
  when I say
  it will
  never
  come to my door

Amryl Johnson

Said by one person.

Children in danger

Tune: Hyfrydol or Blaenwern

See your children, Lord, in danger.
  Lost, alone, away from care.
Move us by your Holy Spirit
  to provide a home to share.
See the battered baby helpless
  and the child at risk today.
Show us how to love your neighbours
  Teach us how to act and pray.

See the addict and the rootless
  On the city's dim-lit street.
Rescue those without a saviour.
  Help us all their needs to meet.
May your Church and all her people
  Parents, children, young and old,
Open hearts and homes to welcome
  Those whose tales can scarce be told.

Fill your people with compassion
  Send them now to those in need.
Save the present generation
  By each prayer and loving deed.
May the Christ who blessed the children
  And received them as his own
Lead us all to live together,
  Bringing hope to those alone.

Dr Martin Eggleton

To be sung before or after the following prayer.

For the children

L: For all children in danger from poverty:
R: Lord, hear our prayer;
L: in danger from homelessness or bad housing:
R: Lord, hear our prayer;
L: in danger from committing crime:
R: Lord, hear our prayer;
L: in danger from drug or solvent abuse:
R: Lord, hear our prayer;
L: in danger from unemployment:
R: Lord, hear our prayer;
L: in danger from sickness and handicap:
R: Lord, hear our prayer;
L: in danger from inappropriate custody:
R: Lord, hear our prayer;
L: in danger from battering:
R: Lord, hear our prayer;
L: in danger from abduction:
R: Lord, hear our prayer;
L: in danger from sexual abuse:
R: Lord, hear our prayer;
L: in danger from neglect:
R: Lord, hear our prayer;
L: in danger from alcohol:
R: Lord, hear our prayer;
L: in danger from marriage breakdown:
R: Lord, hear our prayer;
L: in danger from violence:
R: Lord, hear our prayer;
L: in danger from running away from home:
R: Lord, hear our prayer.

More than enough

I just cleaned my teeth
in more water
than
some babies
drank
today

And yesterday
I rode my bike
more miles
with more thigh
than
some poor kids
will hobble
lamely
from the beginning
of their existence

And before I rode my bike
I had for breakfast
more milk
than
some mothers
have in their breasts
to feed those babies
who had less water
to drink
than
I just cleaned my teeth in
the very same
who will hobble
lamely
less of a distance
than I cycled
after I drank that milk

And a month before this
there were
more than some
who threw
enough
bricks
and burnt enough energy
to build
a fair house
for that mother and son

And the next time it happens
they all will be sprayed
with just a little more water
than
our mother and son
will drink
in a year
though not nearly as much as
the lake of inward tears holds
cried by those
burning
enough
energy
to build
more than enough
houses
for all those kids
who hobble
from the beginning
of their existence

More than enough

*Use one voice, although another voice could read from 'And a month
before this . . .'*

Is the grass greener on the other side?

Our kids throw snowballs
Theirs throw hand-grenades

Ours have snowball fights
Theirs are thrown into battle

We stop our kids going out
so they won't catch a chill

They send their own kids out
and hope they don't get killed

Our kids build sandcastles
Theirs build with sandbags

Ours bury each other in the sand
Theirs are rarely buried

We give our kids
a bucket and spade

Theirs get a gun
and those hand-grenades

Our kids climb trees
Theirs shoot from them

Ours polish their shoes sometimes
They always polish their guns

Our kids learn to count on fingers
Theirs learn to count on bullets

Our kids play Space Invaders
Their kids don't play

Our kids watch videos
of what their kids are doing

Our kids go to school
to read and write

Their kids go to school
to learn to fight

Our kids go off
and come back each day

They hope theirs return
but who can say?

*Mums, Dads, Single Parents or whatever, it's theirs—if the first
two, then Mum or Dad can read 'Our kids' and the other 'Theirs'.*

I can speak with some knowledge . . .

I can speak with some knowledge for those who have once
been married, and now find themselves alone, usually with
children to care for. We are lonely. We are often very tired.
Our sexuality is denied. We even have to listen to the deeply
insulting, 'It's all right for you—you haven't got a husband
to look after.'

It comes as a nasty surprise to be seen as asexual. The
received impression is that giving up sex is seen as
comparable with giving up smoking—very distressing at
first, but gradually one forgets all about it. The reality is
more like giving up food—and no one gets used to
starvation.

From Life Cycle

*Said sensitively by someone who feels this way; or, if that person feels
support is needed, then repeated by three or four people.*

Flag day on the metro

My escalator's rising
and theirs is going down.
I'll gladly be obliging
and give you half a crown.

It pays to help my neighbour live.
My self-esteem's protected.
The more I rise, the more I give,
the less I am affected.

So rattle your collecting tin
and make a great crescendo.
I need your charitable tin
to drown the innuendo

that the stairways are connected.

One person, perhaps dressed for the part.

Prayer—unemployment, despair and dignity

Leader: Gracious God, we lift up against the screen of your
love some of the pain and suffering of your people.

Reader 1: The suffering of the unemployed person who wants
to work, but is left standing in the job market or
dole queue.

Reader 2: The suffering of the student knocking herself out to
get her qualification or master skills for which there
may be no demand—no paid employment available when she is ready.

Reader 1: The suffering of men and women made redundant
after years of work and told that they are now too
old to be re-employed.

Reader 2: The suffering of families adjusting to new

restrictions in spending because the bread winner has become a loser in the economic system we live by.

Reader 1: The suffering of all those deprived of dignity because their identity and value in this society are measured by what they do and not who they are.

Reader 2: The suffering of a worker whose health is ruined for a ridiculous salary.

Reader 1: The suffering of the man who realises he is more than his work, and yet does not know how to find the way to greater fulfilment as a person.

Leader: In all these sufferings, Lord, we see a hunger for love and acceptance—

All: We ask you to help us to love—
to offer love in the attitudes we adopt towards others;
to make love practical—in the steps we take to open up new possibilities for the unemployed and to restore others' dignity;
to receive your love for ourselves—as we claim our place and our value as your sons and daughters— important beyond any of the professional labels we hold or the stigma we bear.
Through Jesus Christ the Lord,
Amen.

Corrymeela Community

Prayer for peace

Lead me from death to life, from falsehood to truth
Lead me from despair to hope, from fear to trust
Lead me from hate to love, from war to peace
Let peace fill our heart, our world, our universe.

One person.

His word

Who are the law makers in our society?
Usually the breakers of His word,
Leaving their graffiti
On walls of decency, making mockery
of morality.
We cannot kill they decree until they give
A uniform to you and me, all in the name
of liberty.
Chosen for us by the state is our enemy
Killing them we become patriots,
Truth is laid beneath blood soaked field
Of dead men.
And we find we are chained to betrayal
My heaving chains bruising mind and soul
Till they cannot be healed.
So do not delegate your conscience
To states and élites,
Save your Amen for your Saviour as you walk
In peace the streets of his world.

Pat Isiorho

A group, perhaps.

A creed

Let us declare our trust in Jesus of Nazareth.

Women:	*Men:*
Child of a carpenter . . .	Calling God Father
One with his people . . .	Creating a new family
Draining the old wine . . .	Fermenting the new
Open to everyone . . .	Narrowing the gate
Deliverer of captives . . .	Binding the free
Bringer of peace . . .	Stirring up strife
Creator of unity . . .	Dividing asunder

Hope for the hopeless . . .	Destroying our hopes
Crucified for all . . .	Compelling cross bearers
Emptying the tomb . . .	Going ahead of us

All:
I trust myself through this Jesus
to the kingdom he points to,
to the God behind it,
in the Spirit who sustains it,
with disciples everywhere who live for it.

Extending or Building the Kingdom

3 into 1 or North meets South

It is often said that politics and religion don't go together, or that we should keep politics out of religion. Of course we cannot align God to party politics but equally we cannot pretend that God is not concerned about the politics of life. The choices we make and the quality of life we create together are God's concern.

How then can we understand the politics of God? A clue lies in the way that we describe God as Trinity. God is three persons gained in an unceasing movement of Love. God is essentially a *community*. Now, having been made in the image of God, our calling is to live like God, that is, to live with and for others in community. We are designed by the creator not as separate but as social beings, to live with rather than over against. Our dilemma was described very clearly by Bishop John Taylor when he wrote: 'God wants us to live life a little below the Angels but our highest ambition is to live a little above the Joneses.' Competition and ambition so often set us over against others and provide us with a standard of living that is far below God's intentions for us.

Many of the writers in this section are speaking of situations of extreme violence and hunger where tens of thousands die every day. Their cry for justice, for community, will only be met when the rich world learns to treat its neighbours as itself.

The threat of death hangs over all equally, however, for Jesus warns that the way God deals with us in some way depends on the way we deal with others (Matthew 22:39).

To read: Luke 16:19–21; also 1 Corinthians 11:17–22.
Has the resurrection convinced us to live differently? Is

your church learning to live as a community? What are the barriers to this?

To reflect: When you read this section think about where on the world map each comes from. If you have time, read up a little on the political situations reflected in the poems. Consider whether and how the mood and the message are different between those which come from the developing world and those from the developed world.

Defeating Darkness

The Lord of history

Group 1:   The Lord be with you

Groups 2,3: And with you

Group 1:   Where two or three are gathered together in his name

Groups 2,3: He is present among them

Group 1:   Let us lift up our hearts

Group 2:   Let us raise them to the Lord

All: Let us give thanks to God

Group 1:   It is right that we should always give thanks to you our God, the Lord of history, who made us after your own likeness and sent your Son to free us from the bondage of sin

Groups 1,2: You have called out of darkness into light
to become a chosen race
a royal priesthood
a holy nation, your own people
to make the world anew according to your will.

All: And therefore we proclaim your good news
to the ends of the earth
and join with all who know your name
to sing of your glory:

Group 1:   Holy, holy, holy, Lord God of hosts.

Group 2:   Your glory fills all heaven and earth.

All: Hosanna in the highest
Blessed is he who comes in the name of the Lord.
Hosanna in the highest.

Response

Reader 1: God, help me to understand the answer Jesus gave
to the question, 'Who is my neighbour?'
About a man on the road who needed help.
About those who refused it—and the one person
who gave it.

Reader 2: Make me more aware that whether I know them or
not, even whether I like them or not, all people
everywhere are my neighbours.

Reader 3: Make me more sensitive to the needs of those I
meet at home, in a shop, along the street,
anywhere.

Leader: Jesus, as we are confronted by the needs of all our
neighbours in this world, may we remember how
you responded to the people you met every day.
May we follow your example and reach out to
others, offering friendship and help in practical
ways. And in so doing, may we discover you in the
neighbours we serve.

Corrymeela Community

Blow your minds on this:

Cimabue crucifixion

Mother and son new-born in isolating grief
bracket the equation of death's display, while
we chat on, establishing the degree, finding
your roots in the quadrate world of kingship
and intricate opulence.

Female in death, from black toe to emphatic
halo, you insinuate presence, monopolising
this moment, in artless condescension to the small
set of man's imagination, blotching the image
more efficiently than Arno.

Your fingers patiently expound the sacramental words, given body and shed blood (in three
precise streams). A crescent torso props the head,
heavy with memories of some
further, latent purpose.

Peter Hackett SJ

One voice.

The centurion

I was on duty last Friday, in charge of crucifixions . . . oh, I
volunteered for it, you see it entitled me to extra leave and
anyway I'd done it before, in fact I was really quite an expert
on the matter. For instance, did you know there are two
distinct types of crucifixion—there's ropes, and there's nails.
With ropes we tie them up there and they take two . . . three
days to die of thirst, exposure. With nails it's a bit quicker
and a lot messier. Friday was a nails job. And there's
another thing people get wrong, you see most folk think the
nails go in here, through the palms of the hands, well of
course if we did that the flesh would tear and he'd fall off the
cross the moment we stood him up. No. In fact they go in
just here, between the two bones of the forearm and you've
got to be careful you don't hit the artery or he'd die in ten
minutes. Of course it's round about there that all the nerves
come into the hand. It's always amazed me just how long
they hang on up there—what with the flogging and dragging
the cross up the hill themselves they usually look half-dead
by the time they get there and it's hard work hanging from a
cross, 'cos you see, when you're hanging from your arms

stretched out like that, you can't breathe. Every time you want to take a breath you have to push up on the nail through your feet, so it alternates see, one minute you're choking to death, the next you can't think for the pain. Still, there's crucifixion for you. And it never really bothered me before, until last Friday. There was a carpenter, oh, a subversive, they said, a dangerous man. There was supposed to be something funny about his trial, I don't know about that, but there was something funny about his execution alright. When we lay him out on the ground to put the nails in, he just accepted it. Usually they kick and shout and scream every curse they can think of at you, well, understandably, but he just lay there. I thought maybe he was unconscious so I shouted something at him —I can't remember what. And he turned towards me. I had to look away. Nobody had ever looked at me like that before, I felt naked, helpless. I was scared. I was scared of a condemned carpenter. When we pulled the crossbar into position, I heard him speak for the first time. I couldn't believe it, I didn't want to believe it, but I could have sworn he was forgiving us. Why? Why couldn't he just curse us and die like everybody else, I could have understood that. I felt sick, I wanted to run away, but I was on duty till sunset, so I stood, shaking, with my back to the cross, keeping the crowds back. Next thing was, about midday the sky went dark; by this time I was in a cold sweat but I wasn't going to run, besides, I'd have been flogged if I had done. But it was dark, no thunder, nothing spectacular, just darkness, like the middle of the night. Then, about half-way through the afternoon, the earth began to shake, and I heard the carpenter shouting above the noise 'It's finished!' I didn't know what I was doing or what I was saying. I fell on my knees and shouted out 'He really was the son of God'. The sky cleared. I looked up, I saw the carpenter. He was dead.

And now they're saying he's risen, his followers. You know, I almost wish it was true, but if it is, even if it isn't, who was he?

Who have I killed? Did he forgive me? I don't know. I
don't know.

Nick McGarvie

One person; needs a good, skilful reader.

This is our God

You are the God of the poor
The human and humble God
The God that sweats in the street
The God of the worn and leathery face
That is why I speak to you
In the way my people speak
Because you are the God the worker
Christ the labourer

One voice.

Jesus is good news . . .

Jesus is good news to all the poor:
hungry, scorned, oppressed or unemployed—
'God will make a world that gives you more:
food, and hope, and life to be enjoyed.'

Power and money, having much to lose,
crucified the love that shook their thrones.
Jesus, raised by God, repeats the news.
Apathy and death are overthrown.

Jesus shouts the gospel from the poor:
'Love will make a world that's good and free.
Leave your gods of money, pomp and power.
Join the struggle, hope, and follow me.'

Brian Wren

The speech statements to be said by someone other than the reader.

We have been offered pie in the sky . . .

We have been offered
pie in the sky
but never smelled it,
neither will it appease
our hunger for rights
that are rightfully ours.

We watch through the window
as you sit feasting
at a table loaded with equality
and grow frantic at its flavour.
How long can we contain
the rumble of hunger in our belly?

James Matthews

A group of people to read this.

Ten commandments for survival

1. We will have no other world but this.
2. We will not raise hopes of life on other plants to which we could escape. What we do now will affect the future, from country to country and planet to planet, from galaxy to galaxy, even to the furthest constellations. For the pollution of one place will be visited upon another and the soundness of one place will benefit the whole universe.
3. We will not speak lightly of the human.
4. We will remember to allow for fallow times.
   There is a rhythm of withdrawal and return in the universe, which we disturb at our peril.
5. We will honour those who have built, planned and worked for the good we enjoy.
6. We will not destroy the earth.
7. We will not pervert the forces of creation.
8. We will not waste or plunder the resources of the world.

 9. We will not justify exploitation.
10. We will not create for ourselves unreal needs.
    We will love the world in its variety and abundance
    and work for its future with our utmost powers. We
    will care for the community of humankind.

Caryl Micklem, (SCM)

Ever since I was born

Ever since I was born
Everyone's been complaining
how the cost of living
just keeps soaring:
Tea from Ceylon
Rice from Burma
Coffee from Brazil
Sugar from Jamaica
Butter from New Zealand
Meat from the Argentine.
Yes, there's no denying
the cost of living
has been rising
ever since I was born.

Yet I haven't heard
a single complaint
since the day I arrived
how the price of human lives
has been taking a nose-dive:
in Hiroshima,
    Stalin's Russia,
        Hitler's Reich,
in Vietnam,
    Kampuchea,
        Uganda,
            South Africa,
                Guatemala,
                    El Salvador . . .

Ever since I was born
the cost of living
has been getting rather steep.
The cost of a life
has never been cheaper.

Cecil Rajendra

One voice.

If time heals

Chorus:	*Poet:*
If Time Heals	Why do people die?
If Death Heals	Why do people cry when someone dies? Is youthfulness a lie?
If Time Heals	Babies must have a near fatal disease slowly but miraculously cured by ageing
If Death Heals	The sicker the better—and like senility must be one hell of a blessing
If Time Heals	How come health came before the Fall?
If Time Heals	What's wrong in the first place?
If Time Heals	Who can be healed in no time at all?
If Time Heals	What's happened to your face?
If Time Heals	Why have we progressed from sticks and stones to atom bombs?
If Time Heals	Why do so many people look back instead of on?
If Time Heals	Why do my shoes wear out?
If Time Heals	Who needs a dog?
If Time Heals	How can Hell be never-ending?
If Time Heals	All we need is more patience
If Time Heals	Why does my watch need mending?
If Time Heals	We preach a Gospel of Clocks
If Time Heals	Is Hour God Minute and Secondary?
If Time Heals	Was Jesus wasting His?

But If Jesus Heals Have You Got The Time?

The kingdom of right relationships

The Kingdom of God is a kingdom without weapons,
 without oppressive powers,
 without torture, without hunger,
 without exploitation of individuals and peoples,
 without racism,
 without an irresponsible use of goods God has given to us.

It is a kingdom full of life,
 faith, justice, peace, love,
 of correct distribution of production,
 of real possibilities for every human being.

That is what we should look towards
 and we have no right as Christians
 to settle for anything else.

AMEN

Christian Conference of Asia

*One voice for the first line of each of the first two stanzas, other voices
for the next lines, or a group to say them in each of these verses. All to
say the last verse.*

The effect of usual behaviour

The effect of usual behaviour becomes amplified through
large systems to a magnitude not encountered before. Usual
family life leads via a worldwide medical system to a
population explosion. Strict educational systems lead to
indoctrination of whole continents. Economic and monetary
systems amplify selfishness to gigantic proportions.

Lutheran World Federation, 1976

One voice.

Solidarity

They followed us in the night,
they corralled us
leaving us no defence but our hands
united with millions of united hands.
They made us spit blood,
they lashed us;
they filled our bodies with electric charges
and our mouths with mime:
they left us at night among the wolves,
they threw us in timeless dungeons,
they tore out our nails!
Our blood covered their rooftops
and their very faces,
but our hands
are united to millions of united hands.

A small group to say this.

Christian hope

One voice.

I understand you, Christ,
because I know betrayal and the spear,
because, like you, I say
I am king and claim my crown.

I ask to be monarch of my own destiny
and father of all children,
I desire emancipation for myself and brothers.

I demand a sceptre for a poor and earthly kingdom,
but dignified and free,
built by the brotherhood of creative hands
in a community of equality and historic prophecy.

That sceptre is mine and I claim it today,
because what I stand for is greater
than the cross I carry,
because my cheeks are tired of the Pharisee's blows
and my arm is asking for the whip.

And when the whir of my whip is silent
and the temple empty of merchants,
then the thorns, the hate and the vinegar,
the scoffing and weeping will be changed into
a welcome to the repentant centurion,
into kindness, poetry and work,
because the man brought back to life
is always incarnating himself in his children . . .
and Christian hope has the face of a child.

Poem by a political prisoner in a Chilean concentration camp.

For our sisters and brothers

God of our daily lives
we pray for the people of the cities of this world
working and without work;
homeless or well housed;
fulfilled or frustrated;
confused and cluttered with material goods
or scraping a living from others' leavings;
angrily scrawling on the wall;
lonely or living in community;
finding their own space
and respecting the space of others.
We pray for our sisters and brothers,
mourning and celebrating—
may we share their suffering and hope.
Amen.

Jan Pickard

To be said by all.

His active and healing peace

Almighty God, all the kingdoms of the world are yours. Grant that the people of * may acknowledge your rule in their own lives and in their country. May your Church deal compassionately with all who suffer because of the activities of terrorists or because of economic ills. Give peace and stability and, above all, a sincere desire to learn and to walk in your way of reconciliation and love.

*In its original form * is replaced by 'Ireland'. Please insert the country/place, as you wish.*

Manual of the Methodist Church Overseas Division.

For all.

'His way' churches

Give us, O Lord, churches
that will be more courageous than cautious;
that will not merely 'comfort the afflicted' but 'afflict the
    comfortable';
that will not only love the world but will also judge the world;
that will not only pursue peace but also demand justice;
that will not remain silent when people are calling for a voice;
that will not pass by on the other side when wounded
    humanity is waiting to be healed;
that not only call us to worship but also send us out to
    witness;
that will follow Christ even when the way points to a Cross.
To this end we offer ourselves in the name of him who loved
    us and gave himself for us. Amen.

From the Christian Conference for Asia, 1977

One voice.

The thirty-seven storey parallel

The waiter who brought the food up to the small and luxurious penthouse dining room wondered what outfit he was serving. Probably the religious group, and the tip would be tiny in spite of the expensive meal.

Like most of the hotel personnel he was grumpy. An ancient joke had been going its rounds: the crowd in the hotel had arrived with the Ten Commandments in one hand and a ten pound note clutched in the other, and neither had been known to be broken . . . the pickin's were pretty slim.

As he set out the food his ears picked up scraps of the conversation. 'If we are going to get any money, we will have to spend plenty of it.' Across the table another commented, 'You've got to have the sugar if you want to attract the flies.' When someone else offered, 'It's not flies we want', no one was listening.

The waiter's temper improved when a handsomely groomed man, who seemed to be in charge of the session, slipped him a sizeable new note for a bit of special service. Was the polished gentleman an interloper among the divines?

The waiter soon realised he would not succeed in getting the dishes cleared before whatever speech-making there was to be got started. The personable fellow was obviously too efficient to allow any awkward lapses. The waiter was right, but he did not mind waiting; the tip was already generous.

'Now let me show you how my organisation can help your church put over its crusade. You know,' he became ingratiatingly confidential, 'this is just the kind of assignment my organisation likes to undertake. What you are doing is good for the people you do it to. That is wonderful. You know, once in a while I have to sell a product I am not sure is the best for the people who purchase. But it's different with what I'll help you sell; it is good for the people.'

Most of those present nodded their heads in solemn agreement. They agreed that what they had was good for the people.

'And if we can persuade people to buy what is not good for them, think what results we can get when we set them after what they really need!' He was tempted to get even more eloquent, but resisted.

'The best possible approach is to work a simple formula. We've got what they need—salvation. They are before the TV screens and lined up on the postal routes. They ride buses, drive cars, all we need to do is to get them into the churches. I think it can be done.'

He had ready for viewing a series of posters, graphs, charts and film strips. They graphically showed the implications of the formula of People—Churches—Salvation. More charts, graphs and strips demonstrated the proven pull of billboard advertising which the personable gentleman's advertising council would themselves donate to the cause; three national preparedness patriotic organisations were ready to co-operate for they realised that salvation was good for military morale; three Hollywood stars, intoxicated with God as 'an ever lovin' doll', would make spot fillers for use in theatres and on TV. The skids were greased, the wheels were oiled. Britain was ready to buy salvation, not in piddling little lumps, but by the trainload, to mix a metaphor a bit.

Finally the good-looking man closed the session. 'Have you thought', he enquired, 'of the parallels? Here we are in an upper room, in fact, we are a lot more upper than the Twelve, for we are thirty-seven storeys above the group. What a symbol of progress we have! It took the Christians four centuries to win such a backward world as the Roman Empire. Think of what we can do with Britain in twelve months, the length of my contract with you.'

Absentmindedly he scraped off some of the crumbs on the white linen tablecloth before him. A few of them caught on his flannel suit and he flicked them off on the floor, but accidentally upset his tumbler of fruit punch which stained the cloth and dripped on the floor.

'But there is a critical difference between the Jerusalem upper room and ours—here we have nobody named Judas!'

Roger E. Ortmayer

Use different people for the various speech sections.

If only

An amusing—yet prickly—look at the contrast between present-day Christians, and the Early Church.

'Is there any other business, gentlemen?'

The monthly Apostles' meeting had been particularly tiring in view of the controversy that had raged over the proposed appeal for the 'Upper Room Restoration Fund'—and Simon Peter, as chairman, was anxious to bring the proceedings to a close. He was, consequently, rather annoyed when old Bartholomew nervously raised his hand.

'Yes, what is it?' he asked, stifling a yawn.

'D...ddddd do you think, sir,' the old fellow stammered, 'that we should be thinking of doing something for Pentecost?'

'I'm afraid I don't quite follow you, Bartholomew,' replied the chief Apostle. 'Do you mean a special service of some sort?'

'W...wwwwww well, I was thinking that as the city will be crowded with Jewish pilgrims, we might do something of an—er—evangelistic nature.'

Peter frowned uneasily. 'I'm not too sure about this,' he said at last. 'We already have a rather full programme ahead, what with the Sale of Works and the missionary tea parties coming up . . . and we did all have a rather hectic Easter. Still, if you think this is a good idea, we might discuss it further at our next meeting. We may have to form a special sub-committee, you understand!'

Despite reservations that were expressed concerning the financial implications of Bartholomew's suggestion, several

Apostles at the next meeting felt that the idea was basically sound. After a period of preliminary discussion it was decided that an evangelistic meeting would be held in the Upper Room on the evening of the Pentecost celebrations.

For want of a better alternative, it was decided that Simon Peter would serve as preacher. Hand-written posters cordially inviting the people of Jerusalem to attend would be placed throughout the city at strategic positions.

The possibility of placing an advertisement in the *Jewish Chronicle* was discussed, but rejected as being too expensive. Peter agreed, however, to explore the possibility of preparing handbills and 'donkey stickers'.

The musical side of the evening was now considered. Levi, the choir master, stated that his choir was willing to participate.

James, however, said that whilst attending a harvest festival service in Bethany some time before, he had heard a particularly moving rendition of 'Where is my wandering boy tonight?' sung by Mary and Martha, accompanied by their brother Lazarus on the harmonium. He suggested that this would make a suitable item for the Pentecost rally.

The Bible reading was now discussed, several members feeling that in view of the evangelistic nature of the evening it would be advisable to use the modern Greek translation in place of the traditional Hebrew text.

This proposal was strongly condemned by others, who took exception to the known Sadducean tendencies of the scholars responsible for the translation. In any case the Hebrew version had been used for many generations without question, and change was felt unnecessary.

Simon Peter, somewhat tentatively, suggested that as every evangelistic meeting obviously needed a guest celebrity, the apostles might well consider asking Cornelius, the military commandant at Caesarea who was known to have strong religious tendencies, to read the lesson.

At this point, several Apostles, under the leadership of Simon the Zealot, withdrew from the main meeting to form the 'Jerusalem (Reformed) Church' on the grounds that Peter's suggestion constituted a sell-out to Rome!

At length, the programme having been settled, the meeting fell silent. Simon Peter was on the verge of bringing the discussion to a close when John, the youngest Apostle, raised his hand.

Peter scowled. The young son of Zebedee was known to be something of a rebel where questions of Church policy were concerned. Mercifully, he had uttered hardly a word all evening until now.

'Peter,' John began, 'are you sure that this is the right way to evangelise the people of Jerusalem? I mean, does this practice of inviting people to meetings really fulfil the Church's Commission to ''go into all the world''?

'Should we not rather try to understand the people we are trying to reach, and try to meet them on their own ground; in the streets and market places, in the Temple, in their homes and places of employment, in their places of recreation . . . ?'

There was a murmur of disapproval around the room, the older Apostles in particular being apparently shocked by the blatant worldliness of John's suggestion . . . and the matter was pursued no further.

The weeks slowly passed and at length the day of Pentecost dawned bright and clear. Reports indicated that an unprecedented number of pilgrims and tourists were streaming into the Holy City, all approach roads having been jammed since noon the previous day with an endless procession of donkeys, camels, and pedestrians.

The Apostles were confident that a goodly number would respond to the attractive hand-written publicity material that had been distributed on street corners throughout the metropolis, and to the striking banner proclaiming 'PETER'S BACK' which now hung majestically over the entrance to the Upper Room.

Hymn sheets had been printed, refreshments prepared, Mary and Martha had agreed to serve in a musical capacity, and Peter had prepared what he privately considered to be his finest sermon, based upon a particularly challenging text from the Book of Zephaniah.

Peter realised that he was late as he turned in to the pathway leading to the Upper Room, and heard the opening lines of 'Rescue the Perishing' drifting towards him. Trying to make himself as inconspicuous as possible, he slipped through a side entrance on to his allotted space on the platform.

The hymn was over, and James, elected to serve as chairman, was welcoming any visitors worshipping in the Upper Room for the first time.

Peter's eyes drifted over the first few rows of empty seats to the assembled members of his regular Sunday congregation. Not many 'outsiders' were in evidence, although he believed that he recognised the leader of the Church in Antioch sitting in the back row. At last, Peter rose to speak.

'It gives me a great joy to speak to you tonight,' he said. 'I'm sure we have a great blessing ahead of us . . .'

Later, the service having ended, the congregation slowly began to disperse. As Peter sat alone on the platform, quietly meditating, he could hear odd snatches of conversation as they drifted towards him.

'Lovely service, wasn't it, dear?'

'Nice sermon.'

'Who arranged the flowers?'

'Pity there were so few outsiders here tonight.'

'A further indication of the hard-heartedness of our generation.'

Despite his outward enthusiasm, Peter was secretly disappointed. It seemed that nobody wanted to hear the old-fashioned Gospel any more.

Ah, if only he could have lived in the time of Elijah and Elisha, and participated in the Mount Carmel revival . . .

If only he had been among the thousands who had flocked to hear Samuel preach . . .

Now it seemed that, contrary to all previous hopes, the

Christian movement was not destined to spread as quickly as they had all expected!

Graham Hedges

Obviously, cast accordingly!

The 'always' hope

God, it is often difficult to feel any hope. We hear so much bad news. Often situations around us appear to be out of control and we feel powerless to change them. Yet we remember that, when Jesus died on the cross and all appeared hopeless, you raised him to new life. Even death could not defeat you. Instead, you give us hope through his resurrection. May we live this and every day in the knowledge of your love and power, and always grow in hope. Grant us open and expectant hearts. Help us to see and celebrate signs of your power at work in our world today. Then we can begin again and again to live out our hope as your disciples—with confidence, courage and joy.

AMEN

Corrymeela Community

One voice.

Living in the Kingdom:
Introduction

Actions speak louder

Christians are often criticised for being all words and no actions. That jibe—which is sometimes valid—challenges us to ask ourselves: how prepared am I to translate worship into work, to take Sunday's liturgy into Monday's living? How prepared am I to live Bread and Wine, to be broken and poured out for the sake of Christ? In the Last Supper Jesus invited his disciples to do just that and he showed them how . . .

Read: 1 Corinthians 11:23–36. Note in this story (and in the Gospel accounts) the four actions of Jesus: *Receiving, Thanking, Breaking, Sharing.* These actions sum up the way Christ lived and can become for us the 'marks of our discipleship'. To live the life of Christ means learning how to receive, to give thanks, to break and be broken, to share.

To Reflect: On your own or in a group brainstorm these four words—what do you immediately think of when you hear each of these words? Which actions come easier to you? Turn to 'Communion' 1, 2 and 3 on pages 159–60. How do these words help to bring new meaning to the Eucharist and Lord's Supper?

Giving, Receiving, Sharing Relationships

Communion—1

This is my Body which is given for you,
do this in remembrance of Me.

When you give your body to be broken
and kicked and starved by the oppressor
to save your brother—
then you will BE the Body of Christ.

When you give your body to heal, restore, and
give life to you sister,
Then you will BE the Body of Christ.

Do this in remembrance of me.

This life giving cup is my shed blood.

When you give the needy a drink of cold water
you give them life in a cup.

My blood is shed to make sins be forgiven.
Let it wash away resentment, bitterness
and grudges between you.

Do this in remembrance of Me.

Beth Webb

To be said by whoever the gathering deems the right person.

Communion—2

This is my Body which is given for you—
Obediently and lovingly you give Me to your brother
and your sister daily—

but you never let Me give Myself to you.

This is my Blood of the new Covenant—
Obediently and lovingly you share life giving water
with your parched Ethiopian neighbour—
but you never let Me wash the dust
out of your throat.

Beth Webb

Communion—3

What you call the Last Supper
is the Eternal Feast.
It never ended,
It never will.
It only becomes more so.

To be said by whoever is seen as right for consecrating and giving the bread and wine.

Eli, Eli . . .

'Eli, Eli, lema sabachthani?'

Life emptied of all meaning,
drained out in a bleak distress
can share in broken silence
my deepest emptiness

and love that freely entered
the pit of life's despair
can name our hidden darkness
and suffer with us there.

Brian Wren

One person.

Universals

The world
and in the world
a street

In the street a gaslight

Under the light
a shivering child

This is the simple
dimension of the
universe

Michele Naglis

One person.

The pain of self-discovery

The pain
of self-discovery
is worth nothing
unless in finding ourselves
we also find each other.

Barbara Platt, Images

One person.

Take this moment

*This is a hymn from the Iona Community, and we are suggesting its
verses can be used as a prayer of dedication and commitment.*

> Take this moment, sign and space,
> Take my friends around,
> Here among us make the place
> Where your love is found.
>
> Take the time to call my name,
> Take the time to mend
> Who I am and what I've been,
> All I've failed to tend.
>
> Take the tiredness of my days,
> Take my past regret,
> Letting your forgiveness touch
> All I can't forget.
>
> Take the little child in me
> Scared of growing old.
> Help him/her to find his/her worth
> Made in Christ's own mould.
>
> Take my talents, take my skill,
> Take what's yet to be;
> Let my life be yours and yet
> Let it still be me.

As best we can

Heavenly Father, we admit the mistakes of our life which we
cannot undo.
Help us to accept their consequences without bitterness,
and within their limits to see our immediate obedience,
and to act upon it with joy.

Caryl Micklem

One, or the gathering as a whole.

Opening

Leader   How wide is our circle of concern and love?

Reader 1: Sometimes it is drawn tightly around myself, quietly keeping others out.

Reader 2: Sometimes it is large enough to take in only my own family and friends—those I call 'loved ones'.

Reader 3: Sometimes it is a circle drawn around my estate, my religious tradition, my political tradition, my country, my race.

Reader 1: Why are you asking? How wide should the circle we care for be?

Corrymeela Community

God of our daily lives

We pray for the people of the cities of this world
working and without work;
homeless or well housed;
fulfilled or frustrated;
confused and cluttered with material goods
or scraping a living from others' leavings;
angrily scrawling the writing on the wall;
lonely or living in community;
finding their own space
and respecting the space of others.
We pray for our sisters and brothers,
mourning and celebrating—
may we share their suffering and hope. Amen.

Jan Pickard

To be said by all.

We are invited

Lord Jesus Christ,
we love to celebrate
the joy of weddings
birthdays
and successes . . .
To meet around a table
and share food and news,
to give and receive presents.
You said,
'The kingdom of God is like that!'
The Kingdom is among us . . .
Here and now, people of every race
and age group
are set free by your cross,
forgiven,
liberated from selfishness,
prejudice
and insularity.
People from every part of the world
are released
from all that divides and separates
to form a new community
enjoying one another's company,
listening to
and receiving from one another
at the great feast God has prepared.
Never before
have there been such opportunities
for meeting
and being enriched by the infinite variety
God has given to creation.

Yet, you reminded us
of those who declined the invitation!
Preoccupied with property,
possessions,

their own little world,
even family life . . .
'We haven't time!'
they said.

Teach us to make time
to go on building up relationships
with others who are invited
to celebrate God's feast.

Maureen Edwards

For all.

Jesus shared our humanity

Leader: Lord, you shared our humanity. You were a baby crying, a child looking for love, a young man at work, a son aware of your mother's suffering. You had to face the criticism of people who didn't understand you. You knew the pain of scorn and rejection. You even shared our death.

People: You also basked in the richness of daily life and events. Your relationships were full of emotion and life. You understood, accepted, cared for and cherished those whose lives came into contact with your own—whether they were women you met drawing water at the well, lepers along the roadside, or children longing to be noticed and hugged.

Leader: So often we deny our humanity and make little of our relationships. But you said, Lord, that you came to give us back our humanity and teach us again what it means to be fully alive.

People: Save us from false and sterile living. Teach us again what it means to embrace and celebrate life every day. Teach us also to relate to each person we meet in such a way that we may find you in each other.
AMEN

Corrymeela Community

Prayers of confession

Leader: Father, to look at Christ is to realise our many failings. Christ was patient—always ready to listen, always ready to talk.

Response: LORD, TEACH US TO BE PATIENT.

Leader: Christ was at home everywhere, with everyone—including the lepers of society.

Response: LORD, HELP US TO BE OPEN TO ALL.

Leader: Christ was not misled by labels or slogans—he met people.

Response: LORD, HELP US TO MEET THE PERSON BEHIND THE MASK.

Leader: Christ was the incarnation of love—he gave himself.

Response: LORD, HELP US TO LIVE FOR OTHERS.

Leader: Christ preached what he lived.

Response: LORD, MAY OUR DEEDS SPEAK.

Leader: Christ carried no grudges—forgives us all.

Response: LORD, FORGIVE US AND TEACH US TO FORGIVE.

Leader: Christ suffered and died for the world.

Response: LORD, GIVE US THE COURAGE TO COMMIT OURSELVES TO LIVE FOR HUMANKIND.

All: WE ASK THIS IN CHRIST'S NAME.

AMEN.

Adapted from Litany of Penance from Ashram

Prayers of confession

God, we confess that we have turned our backs on the unity you desire and have allowed all kinds of divisions in your Church and your world.

We have been unduly proud of our own traditions and scornful of others.

We have emphasised our differences rather than what we have in common. We have not made the effort to understand

those whose beliefs and practices differ from our own, nor
have we been open to what we may learn from other
traditions.
We have also allowed differences of age, gender, colour,
class and nationality to fragment your Church and your
world.
Forgive our arrogance, narrowness and strife, and in your
mercy grant once more the gift of unity to your people.

AMEN

Corrymeela Community

To be said by all.

Kingdom: Past, Present, Future: Introduction

'Now—but not yet'

Jesus's teaching about the future offers at least two different sets of pictures. One group of parables sees the Kingdom slowly but surely growing in our midst, so that despite all the signs to the contrary (wars, hunger, violence and oppression) justice will one day rule the earth again. A second group of parables talks about the kingdom of God breaking in suddenly. At this time the earth as we know it will come to an end, all people will be judged, and a new heaven and a new earth will come into being.

In spite of the differences in these two images, both equally encourage us to 'live the future now' or 'anticipate the future' by living under the rule of God now.

To read: Sort out which parables belong to Group 1 and which to Group 2: Luke 13:5–9; Matthew 13:24–31; Mark 4:26–29; Mark 4:30–34; Matthew 13:47–52.

To reflect: 'We are invited' and 'Lord whether you come as judge' can be used for meditating on the two pictures. Notice how the two are held in tension in both prayers. Or listen to the Jon and Vangelis song 'I'll Find My Way Home'* . . . how does he understand our journey to the future?

'I'll Find My Way Home' was a British chart hit in 1981 but is no longer available through normal channels. It may be found in shops specialising in second-hand records, or 'golden oldies'. See also, in the same way, the album The Friends of Mr Cairo.

Journey, Future, Second Coming, End

To every generation

This is a song lyric by Bill Batstone and can be found on Debby Boone's album Friends for Life *(Lamb and Lion Records).*
*   It seems to us that it can be easily and rather simply adapted for spoken use in a worship gathering.*

Group 1:   From the dawning of the world and its wonders
Before the mountains reached the sky
From everlasting to everlasting
You were there through all time

Group 2:   All my Fathers* heard Your call
Through the ages
They made the choice to follow You
You were faithful
They found Your promise to be true

All:
You have been a shelter, Lord
To every generation, to every generation
A sanctuary from the storm
To every generation, to every generation, Lord

Group 3:   I** was born into Your arms, O my Father
There's still a refuge there for me**
From my** first breath
Drawn from Your breath
You've been my** security

All:

You have been a shelter, Lord
To every generation, to every generation
A sanctuary from the storm
To every generation, to every generation

Group 1:   My** years go before Your eyes
              Like days rush into the night
              Time would steal every dream I feel
              Give my hope a place to hide
              All the days of my** life

Group 2/3: Let my** children know Your mercy in the
                morning
              And find Your greatness as they grow
              May Your glory be their glory
              May Your heart become their home

All:

And You will be a shelter, Lord
To every generation, to every generation
A sanctuary from the storm
To every generation, to every generation
Yesterday, now and forever

*   *We suggest the addition of 'Mothers'.*
** *The use of 'me' and 'my' might be replaced by 'us' and 'our';*
although there can be point and purpose in using the personal with the
awareness that it is said with others communally.

You might also play the album track before or after.

The constant welcome

All: LORD,
        Whether you come as Judge
        or as our King of Glory,
        let us greet your coming
        gladly;

for your judgement will be worked out
in mercy,
and your kingly rule
in love.

We lift our heads to greet you,
and we bring ourselves and our possessions
to be the means by which your love
and mercy are proclaimed;
in the name of Jesus Christ our Lord.

A new creed

We believe in one world,
Full of riches meant for everyone to enjoy.
We believe in one race,
The family of humankind,
Learning to live together by the way of self-sacrifice.
We believe in one life,
Exciting and positive,
Which enjoys all beauty, integrity and science,
Uses the disciplines of work to enrich society,
Harmonises with the life of Jesus
And develops into total happiness.

We believe in one morality: love,
The holiness of sharing the sorrows and joys of others,
Of bringing people together as true friends,
Of working to get rid of the causes of poverty, injustice,
    ignorance and fear;
Love: the test of all our thoughts and motives.
Love: which is God forgiving us, accepting us, and making
    us confident under the Holy Spirit's control.

We believe in Jesus, and the Bible's evidence about him,
Whose life, death and resurrection prove God's permanent
    love for the world,

Who combines in himself life, love, truth, humanity, reality
    and God,
Saving, guiding, reforming and uniting all people who
    follow the way.

We believe in the purpose of God
To unite in Christ everything, spiritual and secular,
To bring about constructive revolution in society, individuals
    and nations
And to establish world government under his loving
    direction.

Subir Biswas

*To be said by all; or, as in some previous suggestions, use a variety of
people but identified by the variety of their jobs, interests and
community associations.*

What is hope?

Leader: What is hope?

Reader 1:   Hope that is seen is not hope. For who 'hopes' for
              what is seen? If we hope for what we do not see,
              though, we actively wait for it with patient
              endurance.

                                        (Romans 8:24–25)

Reader 2:   'To hope means to be ready at every moment for
              that which is not yet born, and yet not become
              desperate if there is no birth in our lifetime. There
              is no sense hoping for that which already exists, or
              for that which cannot be.
              Those whose hope is weak settle down for comfort
              or for violence;
              Those whose hope is strong see and cherish all
              signs of new life and are ready every moment

to help the birth of that which is ready to be
born.'

(Erich Fromm)

Corrymeela Community

The sign

How long, the silence
of so much dry-eyed sorrow?
over this sterile surface
over this piece of desert
they raised an enormous signpost:

Here sorrow has no form, no colour
Life is a pile of stones
White
and dry
Time is a succession of minutes
not yet born
And a cry is an echo
from emptiness to emptiness

Michele Naglis

*A group statement; or by one person with some kind of visual portrayal
or mime.*

Love prayer to Jesus

Love
my heart beats faster
as I run the race You have begun
We run together
and when I am tired You wait
a ray of sunshine resting on my shoulder
or a patch of blue shining through

Love
on this path I meet others
who know You, share You, care for You,
as I do
I can't get enough of their sweetness
Your Name on their lips as holy wine
tasted and good
Together a song, eyes dark lit by
heaven's stars
hope shines
'don't be afraid'
for a future filled with Your light
amid pain, suffering, anguish, weeping,
'don't be weary in well doing'
You lead, You touch, You heal,
stretching us, enabling us to do that
hardest thing

So, in every cell in motion, yet sublimely
at rest, burning with devotion,
we meet the test,
and touch, and flame a little brighter
for having been together IN YOU and WITH YOU,
until, no longer strangers, we pass
that moment, ever alive,
ever sharing, glowing heaven's depths of quiet
Love
Now and always

Sarah Hornsby

One person.

Awaiting dawn

Thy beauty borrows my senses,
Imprinting melodies
Wistful yet calm.

Like languidly waking flowers
Thy pearly parts revolve,
Mine shuttered shiny eyes
Greeting their grace.

For flimsy fractions of beguiling time
Sweet odours overwhelm—then pass away.
Thieves in the naked night.

Remembered phrases forge
Unbidden to the forefront of my stage
Pledging fulfilment real in phantom form.

And deep within the peace of dreamy shapes
Runs life's immortal rhythm.

Yahanan Ramari

One person.

Psalm 20th century

Some people trusted in chariots and horses
Some people trust in missiles and guns
Some people trust in peace-keeping forces
Some people trust in radiation

Don't put your trust in horses and chariots
Said David the Father to one of his sons
who then went and built himself chariot-cities
Untrusting, defensive, so great Solomon?

Some people trust in CND
Some people are satisfied trusting in Christ
Some hedge their bets and trust in Pax Christi
Others trust no one—deterrents suffice

Give me an update on chariots and horses
My horse is no more than my means of deliverance
Give me a chariot, gives me protection
gives the impression, improved circumstance

Some put their trust in cross your heart brassieres
Some people trust being glued to a plank
Most put their trust in blue and red paper
Call me a poet but don't call me crank

Some people trust in reincarnation
Some people trust in reincarnation
Some people trust in reincarnation
And come back as an echo

Some people trust in reincarnation
Some people trust that their works get them through
Some trust in Christ and rest in salvation
Some hope for nothing—nothing will do

Some people trust there really is no God
Some people trust not knowing alright
Some people trust they're bigger than God
and spend their whole life going down with a fight

*Have four people read a line each of the 'Some' stanzas and then repeat
all together. Have one voice to read verses two and four.*

Live his way

Lord, we are attracted and challenged by the kingdom you
proclaim. Often, what you called 'blessed' confuses us. Yet,
we are pilgrims who want to enter your kingdom more fully.
As we journey on, grant us ears to hear your voice, eyes to
see your signs, and hearts and minds open to live by your
values.

Amen

Corrymeela Community

To be said by all.

The One who will

There will be those who are leaders . . . and those who are listeners . . . those who are anxious and those who are critical. There will be those who would prefer to 'stay as they always have been', and those who look to the future with excitement. There will be people of other denominations and cultures, strangers and those who have just come for a look. And at the centre of the 'umbrella' is the One who holds us all together.

The One who will feed and sustain us,
The One who will encourage and lead us,
The One who will make peace between us and reconcile our differences,
The One who will bring us to new understandings and take us in new directions,
The One who will continually remind us to put our trust in Him
and He will supply our every need,
Our Host, our Brother, our Friend, our Master, our Shepherd, our Risen Lord.
And from this centre we shall all be fed and stimulated and inspired . . . to serve and to be served.

He will open our minds to deepen our commitment.
He will open our eyes to see the needs around us.
He will open our ears to hear the cries of the world.
He will open our hearts and equip us to respond.

Rosemary Wass

Have the gathering as a whole to say the indented lines, e.g. 'The One who . . .', 'He will open . . .'

The rebel

I am come of the seed of the people, the people that sorrow,
That have no treasure but hope,
No riches laid up but a memory
Of an Ancient glory.
My mother bore me in bondage, in bondage my mother was
   born,
I am of the blood of serfs;
The children with whom I have played, the men and women
   with whom I have eaten,
Have had masters over them, have been under the lash of
   masters,
And, though gentle, have served churls;
The hands that have touched mine, the dear hands whose
   touch is familiar to me,
Have worn shameful manacles, have been bitten at the wrist
   by manacles,
Have grown hard with the manacles and the task-work of
   strangers,
I am flesh of the flesh of these lowly, I am bone of their bone,
I that have never submitted;
I that have a soul greater than the souls of my people's
   masters,
I that have vision and prophecy and the gift of fiery speech,
I that have spoken with God on the top of His holy hill.

And because I am of the people, I understand the people,
I am sorrowful with their sorrow, I am hungry with their
   desire:
My heart has been heavy with the grief of mothers,
My eyes have been wet with the tears of children,
I have yearned with old wistful men,
And laughed or cursed with young men;
Their shame is my shame, and I have reddened for it,
Reddened for that they have served, they who should be free,
Reddened for that they have gone in want, while others have
   been full,

Reddened for that they have walked in fear of lawyers and of
  their jailors
With their writs of summons and their handcuffs,
Men mean and cruel!
I could have borne stripes on my body rather than this
  shame of my people.

And now I speak, being full of vision;
I speak to my people, and I speak in my people's name to the
  masters of my people.
I say to my people that they are holy, that they are august,
  despite their chains,
That they are greater than those that hold them, and
  stronger and purer,
That they have but need of courage, and to call on the name
  of their God,
God the unforgetting, the dear God that loves the peoples
For whom He died naked, suffering shame.
And I say to my people's masters: Beware,
Beware of the thing that is coming, beware of the risen
  people,
Who shall take what ye would not give. Did ye think to
  conquer the people,
Or that Law is stronger than life and than men's desire to be
  free?
We will try it out with you, yet that have harried and held,
Ye that have bullied and bribed, tyrants, hypocrites, liars!

Patrick Pearse

Different people for the 'I's', or one reader only.

Creation

'Who are you?' asked the Prime Minister, opening the door.
  'I am God,' replied the stranger.
  'I don't believe you,' answered the Prime Minister.
'Show me a miracle.'

And God showed the Prime Minister the miracle of birth.

'Pah,' said the Prime Minister. 'My scientists are creating life in test tubes and have nearly solved the secret of heredity. Artificial insemination is more certain than your lackadaisical method and by cross-breeding we are producing fish and mammals to our design. Show me a proper miracle.'

And God caused the sky to darken and hailstones came pouring down.

'That's nothing,' said the Prime Minister, picking up the telephone to the Air Ministry. 'Send up a met. plane would you, old chap, and sprinkle the clouds with silver chloride crystals.' And the met. plane went up and sprinkled the clouds. The sky darkened the world and the hailstones poured down.

'Show me another,' said the Prime Minister. And God caused a plague of frogs to descend upon the land.

The Prime Minister picked up his telephone. 'Get the Min. of Ag. and Fish,' he said to the operator, 'and instruct them to procure a frogkiller as myxomatosis killed rabbits.' And soon the land was free of frogs, and the people gave thanks to the Prime Minister and erected laboratories in his name.

'Show me another,' sneered the Prime Minister. And God caused the seas to divide.

The Prime Minister picked up his direct-link-telephone to the Polaris submarine. 'Lob a few ICMs into Antarctica and melt the ice-cap, please, old man.'

And the ice-cap melted into water and the sea came rushing back.

'I will kill all the first-born,' said God.

'Paltry tricks,' said the Prime Minister. 'Watch this.' He pressed a button on his desk. And missiles flew to their pre-ordained destination and H-bombs split the world asunder and radioactivity killed every mortal thing.

'I can raise the dead,' said God.

'Please,' said the Prime Minister in his cardboard coffin, 'let me live again.'

'Why, who are you?' asked God, closing the lid.

Brian Morris from Crisis 4

One voice for PM, the other for God.

Can man survive?

In the last fifty years, we human beings have slaughtered by our own hands coming on for one hundred million of our species. We all live under constant threat of our total annihilation. We seem to seek death and destruction as much as life and happiness. We are as driven to kill and be killed as we are to live and let live. Only by the most outrageous violation of ourselves have we achieved our capacity to live in relative adjustment to a civilisation apparently driven to its own destruction. Perhaps to a limited extent we can undo what has been done to us, and what we have done to ourselves. Perhaps men and women were born to love one another, simply and genuinely, rather than to this travesty that we can call love. If we can stop destroying ourselves we may stop destroying others. We have to begin by admitting and even accepting our violence, rather than blindly destroying ourselves with it, and therewith we have to realise that we are as deeply afraid to live and to love as we are to die.

R. D. Laing, The Politics of Experience *(Penguin, 1967)*

One voice.

Testing ground

She spoke of her Pacific Island:
Great stretches of golden sand
Palm tree
Blue sea
And sun,
Always the sun where her people were happy.

Then the white flash, the deafening thunder,
And soap powder falling, falling,
Out of the darkened sky,
And children playing who wondered why.

She spoke of dying crops,
The poisoned fish,
The creeping sickness and the indescribable births.

We listen with the silence of the dumb,
Her gentle voice cuts like a knife.
Our hearts are stone because we dare not feel.

We could not speak,
She it was who said
'It could be your turn next.'

Ruth Cowhig

Use women; one voice until 'We listen', then a group of women.

The (latterday) story of NOAH

God looked upon the earth, and behold, it was corrupt, and
the earth was filled with violence. And it repented the Lord
that he had made man on the earth, and it grieved him at his ·
heart. And the Lord said: 'I will let this man whom I have
created destroy himself: he shall also destroy beasts and
creeping things and the fowls of the air.'

And it especially grieved the Lord that even the power to
choose a remnant had been arrogated to mankind, for that
men had chosen their own remnant, and those with power
had chosen themselves; and they had anticipated the Lord in
his suggestion that they make them an ark. (But, verily, the
Lord knew better than that they should triumph.)

Those who had usurped the power of the Lord and had
built unto themselves an ark were of the faith that
the Nuclear Option Advanceth Harmony, which being

abbreviated is NOAH. Verily they were few in number, being of government, local authority or military stature only.

And behold, the Lord observed how that NOAH built an ark: viewless, and beneath the earth, of reinforced concrete within and withou t. And many rooms there were, decked out with computers and microfilm of those likely to cause a breach of the peace (daughters of the gods at Greenham, and Communists, Nihilists and Defeatists, which are called CND), and with telecommunications systems, yea, and disinfectant, tinned foods and jars of peanut butter.

And God did not try to interest NOAH in taking aboard things of all flesh, two of every sort, male and female—or fowls after their kind, and of cattle after their kind, of every creeping thing of the earth after his kind, to keep them alive—for he knew that it was all vanity. But NOAH of his own desire took a few fowl, that animal exploitation might continue unabated.

And behold, mankind committed the ultimate sin in the eyes of the Lord, and all the fountains of the great deep were opened up, and also the windows of heaven; and great was the blast and abominable the destruction thereof. And all flesh died that moved within the northern hemisphere, both of fowl, and of cattle, and of beast, and of every creeping thing that creepeth upon the earth, and every man: all in whose nostrils was the breath of life, of all that was in the northern hemisphere, died. And every living substance was destroyed which was upon the face of the earth; and NOAH only remained alive, and the fowls that were there in the ark.

And there expired many days, and the wind that passed over the earth served only to increase the devastation, carrying the abominable substances into the southern hemisphere.

And in the third month NOAH released a raven, which went forth to and fro. And also a dove was sent forth to see if the fallout was abated from off the face of the ground, but it was not. And the dove returned unto NOAH in the ark, and NOAH put forth a hand and pulled her in unto a decontamination bag.

And after many more days NOAH again sent forth the dove out of the ark; and the dove returned in the evening: and lo, in her mouth was a burnt stick encrusted with ice. And NOAH wondered what this could betoken. And after several more days, NOAH again sent forth the dove, which returned not again any more.

And it came to pass that NOAH misread the sign of the dove's disappearance; and did emerge from the ark, and looked. And behold, the face of the ground was a frozen desert, and the dove lay petrified upon the ice outside the ark. And lo, there was no sun; but only darkness and deep cold.

And NOAH despaired of any foodstuff growing again upon the face of the ground, and did groan, having now exhausted the supply of tinned foods and peanut butter.

And the Lord had compassion in his heart for NOAH, but the heart of NOAH had long ago hardened against the purposes of the Lord: winter had clearly come upon the soul of NOAH before nuclear winter came upon the face of the earth. Yet now it repented NOAH that there could have been a weapons-freeze instead of a deep freeze. But it was not so, because man had more love for power than power to love.

And such was the disturbance of the ionosphere that NOAH saw not the bow set in the cloud which the Lord ventured to put forth for an epitaph.

Kate Compston

Divide, as desired, in terms of readers.

Forever now or never

On earth it was August, 1914, but in Heaven, where the Lord God stood looking out of His window at the universe, time is reckoned differently. There it was simply known as the time when the cherubim ordinarily came out to play on the floor of Heaven. But on this occasion not a cherub was in sight, for the Lord God was exceedingly wroth. Lightning crackled around His head, and thunder rolled across the great arch overhead. His Son came hurrying to the window to look with saddening eyes at what was taking place on the minor planet He had once visited. It was an all too familiar spectacle. An army was invading its neighbour's borders, and refugees were streaming down the roads as they had done ever since man had become the dominant creature on that war-torn world.

'I have had enough of this Earth!' the Father cried. The lightning flashed with the fury of His words, and the unhappy cherubim hiding in the corners trembled. Everyone in Heaven caught his breath as the mighty arm of the Lord moved slowly upward in the gesture that would spell annihilation for the offending planet.

The Son grasped the ascending arm gently, staying its awful power. 'Father,' He said, 'forgive these people, for they know not what they do.'

'I have heard you say those very words before,' the Father retorted. 'And I did forgive them. But they continued their evil ways. They are reasonably intelligent creatures—quick enough to learn new means of destruction but slow to learn the ways of righteousness and peace. I have had enough of them!'

'Nevertheless, they are my people,' the Son said. 'I ask you to spare them.'

'Spare them! They are bent on murdering one another!' The thunder rose to a tremendous crescendo that made the cherubim cower. 'My patience is at an end. They have had their chance. When you went among them, they murdered you as they destroy everything good that comes their way.'

The Son held His Father's arm firmly. 'Still, they are my people. As I went among them before, so with your permission, I will go among them again to try to teach them the spirit of brotherhood.'

The Father's anger did not abate. 'This planet is an offence to the most distant star and a constant source of trouble to Heaven. It should be blotted out of existence!'

But the Son shook His head and smiled, seeking His Father's permission to visit His errant people again. Slowly the thunder died away, and anger turned to sadness. 'So be it,' the Father said finally. 'Do as you wish, but I forsee nothing but the re-enacting of an old tragedy.'

The Father turned away, and the cherubim crept timidly out of their corners to play on the floor of Heaven.

And so on Earth there was born a child of parents appropriately named Joseph and Mary, which are common names among the Jews who dwell in the villages of western Poland. The infant survived the war that raged around him for nearly four years; during the peace that followed he grew up among his people to become a leader whose wisdom and goodness had much influence. Nearly everyone loved and respected him, but there were some who feared him for the power he had in his community.

When he reached the age of twenty-five, the armies marched again, darkening the sky with the smoke of burning villages. He was the first to be denounced to the soldiers who came on motorcycles in advance of the lumbering tanks following them down the road. Spies who had been planted in the village called out the names of a dozen of his dearest friends and the thirteen young men were marked for death.

The skies grew black and a great wind howled across the countryside as the little group of men were marched out of the village surrounded by guards carrying machine guns. They were taken to a rocky hill, which had served as an execution place in ancient times, and there the corporal in charge had twelve of them shot without ceremony. But when he came to the thirteenth man, a spy who had followed the firing squad whispered something to him. The corporal grinned and nodded knowingly, looking up at a huge dead tree that stood on the very summit of the hill. He spoke to his men. They seemed taken aback for a moment, but they had been well trained in their profession, so they obeyed him without question.

They started up the hill, driving their shackled prisoner ahead of them. The storm increased its fury, and the soldiers appeared uneasy as they went about carrying out their orders. Finally they had done what they were told to do, and they fled from the hilltop, leaving behind them the crumpled bodies of twelve young men and the still-living figure of a man pinioned to a tree that bent and tossed in the wind which tore at its branches.

No one saw the man die, for the storm was so furious that even the invading army was held up by it for a few hours.

The Lord God was standing at the window when His Son returned. His anger was terrible to behold. Lightning played around His head, and the crash of thunder frightened the sorrowing cherubim. But again the Son pleaded with His Father, and stayed the arm that was ready to hurl annihilation upon the Earth.

'They are my people,' the Son said humbly. 'Twice now I have dwelt among them, and I know the evil and the good that struggles in their hearts. They are a long way from Heaven, so it is hard for us to understand them here. But when I was in their midst I felt for the evil ones among them as well as for the good. Father, I plead with you again to spare them. They are not all bad. I have seen men among them lay down their lives for others; I have seen nobility in their hearts, and a growing desire for peace. For their innocent children, for their women who are capable of great love, and for the occasional man who is trying in his own blundering way to right the wrongs of such a world, I beseech you, Father, to give these people one more chance.'

The stern face at the window softened. 'Very well then, My Son,' the Lord God said at last, brushing the crackling lightning away. 'For your sake I will spare them from instant annihilation. You have suffered at their hands, so you have the right to speak for them.'

The Father's voice went on still shaken by the wrath that burned within Him. 'However, this time I must impose a condition. This time these people's fate must be in their own hands. For I shall now reveal to them the secret that will mean their destruction or salvation. I shall let them discover the innermost secret of the universe and give them the power of tearing apart the atom that is the key to all matter. With this knowledge they must utterly destroy their world or remake it into a place of peace and plenty. It is for them now to decide their own destiny. So be it.' The Father withdrew and left His Son alone.

The thunder died away, and the cherubim came out from their hiding places to play around the feet of the lonely figure at the window whose lips were murmuring a prayer for all the good-hearted men and women He had known on earth.

'In their hands be it,' the cherubim heard Him say. 'Forever now or never. Amen.'

Philip Van Doren Stern

Use various voices, particularly one voice for each of the 'speech' sections.

Why have you abandoned me?

My God, my God, why have you abandoned me?
A caricature have I become
and people despise me.
They sneer at me in all the newspapers.
Tanks surround me,
machine guns take aim at me,
barbed wire, loaded with electricity, imprisons me.
Each day I am being called up,
with a number they have branded me
and behind the grate they have photographed me.
My bones can be counted like on an X-ray sheet,

Naked they push me into the gas chamber
and my clothes and shoes they have shared among themselves.
I cry for morphia, but nobody hears me.
I cry in the fetters of the waistcoat,
in the mental hospital I cry the whole night long,
in the ward for incurable patients,
in the old people's hall for contagiously ill.
In the psychiatric clinic I wrestle perspiring with death.
Even under the oxygen mask I suffocate.
I am in tears at the police station,
in the court of the house of correction,
in the torture chamber,
in the orphanage.
I am contagious with radioactivity
and people avoid me for fear of infection.

BUT I WILL TELL MY BRETHREN ABOUT YOU.
IN OUR MEETINGS I WILL PRAISE YOU.
IN THE MIDST OF LARGE CROWDS MY HYMNS WILL BE INTONED.
THE PEOPLE WHICH STILL HAVE TO BE BORN,
OUR PEOPLE,
WILL REJOICE IN A GREAT FEAST.

Ernesto Cardenal

One voice.

Affirmation

All to say, loudly.

> I will give names
> to life's terrors
> of despair and anguish
> of pain and emptiness

Tony Jasper

*Alternatively, say this in groups of five (or whatever, depending on the
number present), then by quarters (divide the gathering into four) then
by halves (into two!), then say together.*

Praying for Jerusalem

Lord, dear Lord,
I long for Jerusalem;
The city built high in heaven,
but also the one built on the rocks
over there in Israel.

Lord God,
then I would see, in my mind,
how he was pushed and lashed
through city streets to Golgotha
and see there how he died for us . . .
Then Easter
when he rose from the dead.
Rejoicing, dancing and clapping
I would shout:
He is risen!
He is risen!

Prayer by an unknown Ghanaian Christian.

One voice, with the gathering repeating the last two or three lines.

The witnesses

Are they with us?—
these who go from door to door
persistently believing
taking no care to stop and smell the daffodils
lest the end comes suddenly.

Are they with us?—
these in saffron robes with shaven heads,
beating their High Street tambourines,
waking their god
outside the superstore.

Are they with us?—
these carrying candles in Bangor,
selling herbs in Derby,
making money for the guru
in Oldham Market.

Are they with us?—
these fresh-faced lads and gypsy-skirted girls
selling books outside Woolworths
to burdened shoppers.

Do they witness to the same lord
he who calls for passion of obedience
for fire of unremitting faith
who plants the seeds of peace
somewhere close to the soul?

I need to know who walk with us
and talk the language breathed from heaven,
who dance this life before the mystic moon
and stumble in the dark
when the lights go out.

Martin Eggleton

*A group to say the first line, someone to say each of the next lines in
each stanza.*

Prayer written in a Johannesburg prison

Teach us to walk in your presence with ease and not embar-
    rassment.
Guide our thinking and direct our acting so that we may not
    be like strangers calling on you on a rare visit, but rather
    like sons and daughters at home with you.
May we never forget that you do not call us like Moses to
    catch an occasional glimpse of your blinding glory; but
    that ever since you sent your son Jesus Christ to walk this

earth and pitch his tent among us you have invited us to be partners with him and to follow him in the way he himself walked.

It is not a smooth and easy way; the going is rough; but you promise to give us the energy, courage and perseverance to plod on, as long as, once we have put our minds to it, we do not look back and have any regrets.

Father, please go before us, to lead;
   walk beside us, to befriend;
   be above us, to protect;
   stay behind us, to direct;
   be beneath us, to support;
   abide with us, to love. Amen

Jean-Francoise Bill

One voice until 'Father, please go . . .'; then everyone.

Always there

O God,
Giver of life,
Bearer of pain,
Maker of love,
For all that has been, thanks,
To all that shall be, yes,
At all times and in all places.

Silence

Thanks be to God.

One voice, with all saying the final line.

Lord we praise you

Lord we praise you for your people
Who set out on the journey,
The journey of faith which began in your Son.

We sing as we join them and travel together,
As ages and cultures are merged into one.
We all join to sing the praises of Jesus,
We all bring our gifts to honour his name.
   Lord we praise you for the martyrs
   Who died on the journey.
   They laid down their lives to honour your name.
   From their scattered seeds your World Church has ripened,
   And kingdoms and countries were won in your name.
   We all join to sing the praises of Jesus,
   We all bring our gifts to honour his name.
Lord we praise you for the guides
Who mapped out the journey,
Translators and teachers who taught us your way.
Your stories are told as we travel together,
Your love is proclaimed in the tongue of the day.
We all join to sing the praises of Jesus,
We all bring our gifts to honour his name.
   Lord we praise you for the prophets
   Who lead on the journey,
   Your words they have spoken, your power they proclaim.
   In their voices you challenge the forces of evil,
   And through them the nations have learned of your name.
   We all join to sing the praises of Jesus,
   We all bring our gifts to honour his name.
Lord we praise you for the calling
To be on the journey.
The journey of faith which begins in your Son.
With the martyrs and prophets and teachers we travel.
In the steps of the saints we are travelling on.
We all join to sing the praises of Jesus,
We all bring our gifts to honour your Son.

David Hill

To be said by all; but it might be best to have particular groups of people to read the verse and then for all to say the refrain. The 'particular' groups might be reflected in age so that there is given an overall feel of 'journey'.

Litany of the saints

This is said, if convenient, in procession.

Bridegroom of poverty, our brother Francis of Assisi,
follower of Jesus and drop-out, friend of the creation:
Stand here beside us.

Confessors in flames, Norman Morrison, Roger LaPorte,
Jan Palach, Thich Quang Duc and all their companions,
immolated for the cause of peace:

Confessor in Russia, Boris Pasternak, poet of reconciliation:

Confessor in Denmark, Søren Kierkegaard, diver in the
sea of his own soul:

Confessors in America, Henry David Thoreau and Thomas
Merton, hermits and resisters:

Good Pope John, friend of the poor, who longed for the
unity of mankind:

Apostle of non-violence, Gandhi the Mahatma, reproach to
the churches:

Mask of the Christ, Gautama the Buddha, fountain of
compassion:

Peacemaker in America, A. J. Muste, father of activists:

Peacemaker in the world, Dag Hammarskjöld, denier of
himself:

Priest and panhandler, Benedict Joseph Labre, fool for
Christ:

Madman in America, Johnny Appleseed, planter of Eden:

Witness in England, John Wesley, street minister:

Faithful harlot, Mary Magdalen, first witness of new life:

Inductee of Africa, Simon of Cyrene, who carried the cross
of your liberator:

Reformers and preachers, George Fox and Menno Simons,
who founded communities of peace:

Visionary and poet, William Blake, on trip by power of
imagination:

Visionary and apostle, John the Evangelist, resister to the
power of the Beast:

Patrons of healing, Luke the beloved, Louis Pasteur, and
  Florence Nightingale:

Priest and scientist, Pierre Teilhard de Chardin, voyager in
  the past and in the future:

Those who speak the soul's language, Bach, Mozart,
  Beethoven and their brothers:

Peter Maurin, Catholic worker:

Harriet Tubman, black liberator:

Martin Luther, reformer and leader of protest:

Martyrs of Africa: Perpetua, mother; Felicity, slave; and
  your companions:

Martyrs and Confessors, Polycarp, Ignatius and Justin,
  who refused the incense to Caesar:

Martyr in Prague, Jan Hus, reformer:

Holy innocents of Birmingham, in your undeserved deaths:

Victims of lynching, known and unknown, brothers of
  Stephen the martyr:

Victims of Hiroshima and Nagasaki, pierced by needles of
  flame:

Victims of Coventry, Dresden, and Tokyo, caught up in a
  storm of fire:

Victims of Auschwitz and all concentration camps, in your
  despair and death:

Children of Viet Nam, mutilated to preserve a way of life:

Martyrs in the streets of the South, Jonathan Daniels,
  James Reeb, Medgar Evers, Michael Schwermer, and all
  your companions:

Martyrs to the State, Maximilianus and Franz Jägertatter,
  draft resisters:

Martyr in Bolivia, Camillo Torres, priest and
  revolutionary:

Martyr in Germany, Dietrich Bonhoeffer, confessor and
  revolutionary:

Martyr in America, Martin Luther King, organiser for
  peace and justice:

Unwed mother, blessed Mary, wellspring of our liberation:

Our hero and leader, Jesus the prophet, who resisted the
  Establishment:

Our hero and leader, Jesus the Liberator, a king because
   first a servant:
Our hero and leader, Jesus the poet, who laid down a new
   form of speech:
Our hero and leader, Jesus the son of God, bright cornerstone
   of our unity in a new Spirit: STAND HERE BESIDE US.

From A Covenant of Peace: A Liberation Prayer Book

*When I have used this Litany, I have substituted various names for
those given, since some of these are particularly American or possess
direct relevance to American affairs.*

*I have also at some points added; so for instance in the section which
praises 'those who speak the soul's language' I add, Dylan, U2, Joan
Baez, Lennon & McCartney. Some people would of course choose
others. The list need not stop at musicians.*

The litany should be attacked fairly briskly.

The kingdom's call

Lord, we are attracted and challenged by the kingdom you
proclaim. Often, what you called 'blessed' confuses us. Yet,
we are pilgrims who want to enter your kingdom more fully.
As we journey on, grant us ears to hear your voice, eyes to see
your signs, and hearts and minds open to live by your values.
Amen.

Corrymeela Community

Said by all, or by one for the gathering.

In Christ

   In Christ we are free
   hallelujah
   In Christ is our direction
   hallelujah

In Christ is our strength
hallelujah
in Christ is our present
hallelujah
in Christ is our future
hallelujah
in Christ is life beyond this
hallelujah

Tony Jasper

Have everyone read the statements, differing areas of the gathering to respond with 'hallelujah', and then all on the last.

No defeat

As Christians we are not in retreat. We are aware that He is always ahead of us, waiting to be found, known and met. Sometimes we are conscious that we are reclaiming land and territory that has been taken by the forces of darkness.

Let each person read aloud, say aloud, one line at a time and then say together as a group.

No defeat!
We will reclaim the territory
Where the enemy's been moving,
We will fight with authority
With the Holy Ghost and power.
With a God like our God—
What a God is our God!
We cannot, we must not,
We will not know defeat.

Chris Bowater, from Creative Worship.

Litany of new birth

Leader: God of life and birth
People: How you labour, how you suffer, to bring forth the new creation.
Leader: You cry out like a woman in childbirth
People: And the Spirit groans within you.
Leader: But your cries become cries of joy
People: As you behold new life there before you.
Leader: Even a mother might forget us
People: Yet you will not forsake us.
Leader: You will give us a new beginning
People: You will give us a new earth
Leader: There will be no more tears
People: There will be no more sorrow
Leader: There will be no more violence
People: There will be no more death.

Corrymeela Community

The kingship of God

Leader: There is a very old African custom that invokes God's supreme kingship.
Males: I am his
All: I am God's
Females: I am his woman
Males: I am his man
All: He made me
He will judge
and He will watch!
Leader: That kingship of God is our guarantee, hope and security
All: Love is our substance
His love is our substance
It should be our substance, in all and everything
His love is our security
and guarantee

Males: Alleluia
Females: Alleluia
All: Alleluia

Age irrelevant

Old and strong
She goes on and on
You can't kill the Spirit
She is like a mountain

Naomi Littlebear Morena, from Gentle Angry People.

This could be read next to Isaiah 40:28 – 31.

Deathbed

Now, when the frail and finespun
Web of mortality
Gapes, and lets slip
What we have loved so long
Out of our lighted present
Into the trackless dark

We turn, blinded,
Not to the Christ in Glory,
Stars about His feet

But to the Son of Man,
Back from the tomb,
Who built fire, ate fish,
Spoke with friends, and walked
a dusty road at evening.

Here, in this room, in
This stark and timeless moment,
We hear those footsteps

And
With suddenly lifted hearts
Acknowledge
The irrelevance of death.

Evangeline Patterson

For one voice.

Blessings and Commission

Life like this

May the God who dances at creation,
who loves us with human love,
and who shakes our lives like thunder,
be with us all and send us out to fill the world with justice.
Amen.

To be said by the worship leader, or by all, at the end of a service.

All we need is hope

Hope leads everything,
For faith only sees what is,
But hope sees what will be.
Charity only loves what is.
But hope loves what will be—
In time and for all eternity.

Send us out in the power of your spirit
To live and work to your praise and glory.

Amen.

Use two voices on the first stanza, one to lead and the other for lines two, four and six. All, or both the readers, to say the last two lines.

God be in my head

God be in my head,
and in my understanding.
God be in my eyes,
and in my looking.
God be in my mouth,
and in my speaking.
God be in my heart,
and in my thinking.
God be at mine end,
and at my departing.

Celtic blessing

To be said by all.

The new sound

Jesus said
we play dirges and do not mourn,
frantic rock and do not freak out.
A new music must be heard
which will drive us to dance
in a world wrung with flatness.
Tonight will we not all sleep
with one ear in dream
and one alert
    for the crackling of concrete
    and the blossoming of the earth?

To be said before the final blessing, and perhaps at a worship gathering that has been centred around music.

Closing prayer

Lord, let us not wander from your way.
Keep our eyes fixed on you and on our goal.
But let us not travel with such intense concentration on the
    destination that we cannot take time to enjoy the gifts of
    this day.
Teach us to stop and celebrate signs of your kingdom in the
    wonders we see, in the people we meet, in the experiences
    we share.
For we give you thanks for the journey itself, as well as the
    destination we await.
Through Jesus Christ our Lord.
Amen.

Corrymeela Community

To be said by all.

Always with him

Remain with us, O God, and grant us your peace.
There is no strength but in you.
There is no unity, but in your house.
Under your hand we shall pass all danger.
You are our mother and our father.
You are our home. Amen.
May the blessing of the Holy Trinity rest upon us
and upon all our work and worship done in God's name.
And may the grace of our Lord Jesus Christ and the love of
God and the fellowship of the Holy Spirit be with us
all evermore.

Amen.

To be said by the leader, or by all.

Forever peace

The peace of the Lord be with you always.
    A peace that means assurance
    that in our frantic racing
    through a million anxious hours
    we have a bond
    that cannot break,
    for God Himself
    has tied the cords
    of faith and life
    on either end.

One voice.

Go forth in peace

Go forth into the world in peace, have courage, hold fast
what is good, return no one evil for evil; strengthen the faint-
hearted, support the weak, help the suffering; honour all
men and women; love and serve the Lord, rejoicing in the
power of the Holy Spirit.

AMEN

Corrymeela Community

One voice.

An Irish blessing

May the road rise up to meet you
May the wind be always at your back
May the sun shine warm upon your face
    the rains fall soft upon your fields,
And until we meet again, may God hold you in the palm
of his hand.

For all. Let people turn to face each other, as they say this.

To meet him, wherever . . .

Go now, all of you, in peace
to the place
where God has given you responsibility
and he himself will bless you,
the Father, the Son and the Holy Spirit.

For the leader to say.

He is Lord

One word, one shout, one blast—that's all.
No ifs and buts
no high level conferences
no we-will-if-you-wills.
That day will see the summit to beat them all—
God, Father, Son and Holy Spirit,
rolling up the earth and heavens
of this old creation.
No one gave them
permission to start it
they need no permission to end it—
only their own creative love.
The new will be unrolled and all will see
the authority of our one Creator God.
There will be no protest, no discussion,
but all will bow and say that
Jesus Christ is Lord.

Anne Roberts

*Try one voice for 'One word', many voices for the next words until
'. . . you-wills', then different voices until 'old creation'. Back to one
voice until the first group picks up at 'The new will be unrolled' and
runs to 'no discussion'; then everyone, with perhaps the whole
gathering rising to say 'Jesus Christ is Lord'.*

Worship Orders

Preface

For the most part these worship orders do not envisage a regimented service that will commence at 11 or 6.30 and finish a minute or two after the hour's duration. They are intended for gatherings where the Spirit blows where it wills. Naturally we hope the material found in *In Unexpected Places* will be used in more conventional gatherings where, shall we say, the 'hymn-sandwich' operates, and that within this confine it will breathe new life; but here, in the ensuing material, we are anticipating there is a group of people wishing to worship and celebrate in powerful ways. We also assume some, if not all, of this gathering are willing to spend *time* preparing this material and we should expect it to be adapted accordingly.

However, do not think the material flies away into the sunset, for we hope it is rooted in Christian tradition and awareness and indeed from time to time the 'traditional' is advocated.

Obviously it is not easy to choose the 'right' music and in the case of songs and hymns for singing by the gathering we have made great use of *Mission Praise*. Where material lies elsewhere then we have noted the source, but there may be many other sources that contain the same song or hymn. Not every service has 'singing' for indeed there are some Christians who dislike the 'singing' aspect of worship either because it leaves them out in the cold (doubting their own vocal ability!); or because they would gravitate more toward moments of quietness and stillness, and find much modern worship noisy, and sometimes so for no real reason.

These services are offered for use and no more. No claim whatever is made for their greatness. Some parts of most have been used in practice, occasionally the whole. May they make more real the God of our Lord Jesus.

Please be willing to adapt, change, radically alter the following ideas. It is not easy suggesting particular hymns and songs that might be sung, and we have chosen well-known or fairly familiar material. Again, it is not easy suggesting reflective material or non-biblical readings without fetching the comment 'But we haven't got this book'; but so be it! Please take note of 'worship' comments made in the book's introduction.

Worship 1: Seeking the Kingdom

1. Music. Someone plays on the piano 'Abba Father' (*Mission Praise* 1) and does so several times. The gathering hums the tune. One side of the gathering sings the words. Then the other side. Finally all together.

2. All stand. Say together 'He is to be praised' (p. 15) as outlined for leader and gathering.
   Three remain standing: each sings a verse and all sing the refrain from *Praise* (p. 22).

3. All sit. Scripture: Psalm 46:1–3; Matthew 11:28; Matthew 23:27.

4. Comment on Scripture: 'God can only be a compassionate God, loving and suffering with us. That is why the Psalmist can speak as he does. Shelter is a place without fear. Refuge is a place of security. This is our God—the God who not only does not make us fear but removes fear from us. This is the God who speaks to us through Jesus. Jesus' God is the God of compassion.' Choan-Seng Song, *Theology from the Womb of Asia* (SCM Press 1988), p. 146.

5. All sing (standing or seated) 'O Give Thanks to the Lord (*Mission Praise* 182).
   All sing (standing or seated) 'Seek ye first the Kingdom of God' (*Mission Praise* 201). (If seated, then rise for the last refrain and sing twice.)

6. Prayer: 'Standing with Him' (p. 53).
7. Read: 'O God I am chained' (p. 70); read fairly slowly, do not rush.
8. All sing 'How lovely on the Mountains' (popular version, *Mission Praise* 79).
9. Address.
10. Meditation. The preacher/speaker shall have given some lines to, say, five people. These will be repeated, separately, with a space between. People will be asked to hear, think some more, offer prayer or merely take time to dwell on these thoughts.
11. Intercessions. As outlined, say 'Lord you have brought us together' (p. 84). Some shall offer prayers on matters that need attention, as led, though some guidance might be offered and members of the gathering be ready to offer words.
    At some point names of this gathering who need prayers are mentioned.
12. This week. Time for members to reflect on the past week; joys and difficulties in living the Christian life, how God has or has not been encountered (seemingly).
13. Offering for the continuation of the Work (see also 14).
14. While the offering is taken, let a soloist or a choir sing, or use relevant recorded music of the time, taking due care not to rudely interrupt the intent of 1–12. Initially play softly and then increase to moderate volume.
15. Bring forward offering. The leader (or those who have brought the offering forward) can raise the plates so that the gathering is aware. Say together 'Always thanks' (p. 29).
16. Then say whatever version of the Lord's Prayer is desired.
17. All sing 'Now thank we all our God' (in virtually all collections, and to the tune that is desired; or sing Gracias (Beaumont) for verses 1 and 2 (using piano) and verse 3 to Nun Danket (using organ)).
18. Say the Grace together.
19. Play appropriate music, or sing the song with which this began.

Worship 2: Seeking the Kingdom

Dim lights. If appropriate light candles or so use lighting that a central cross is very visible.
1. Music. Philip Bailey, album *Triumph*, track: 'Come before His Presence'.
2. Fade music gently on its own fade.
3. One minute's silence.
4. Someone to say 'He confronts us' (p. 28).
5. Music. Philip Bailey, album *Triumph*, track: 'Marvellous'. (We suggest you do not play the noisy first few seconds.)

Intensify lighting.
6. The Sanctus, as divided (p. 13).
7. All sing 'Majesty' (*Mission Praise* 151).
8. Say 'His will be done' (p. 57).
9. Today in the news: read extracts from the current newspapers (try and form a varied collection ranging from politics to sport, human interest to pop).
10. Read Seeking the Kingdom: Introduction (p. 45).
11. Scripture. Matthew 20:1–16.
12. All sing 'Will You Come and Follow Me' (Iona Community), or 'For the Healing of the Nations' (*Methodist Hymns and Psalms*) or 'O Lord the Clouds are Gathering (*New Songs 1987/8 Music Book*, Kingsway).
13. Prayers on the topics raised for 9. Sing between each petition either 'Someone's crying Lord, Kum Ba Ya', or the verses of 'He is Lord, He is Lord' (either arrangement *Methodist Hymns and Psalms* 256 or *Mission Praise* 69) or refrain of 'Jesu, Jesu, Fill us with your Love (*Methodist Hymns and Psalms* 145).
14. If 'Jesu, Jesu' is used, then here sing the complete song; or do so anyway!
15. Address/sermon/visual presentation illustrating points raised by 10.
16. Song 'I walked through the lonely streets' (Iona Community).
17. All sing 'I Trust in Thee O Lord' (*Mission Praise* 85), or

Mother Teresa's 'Daily Prayer' (*Partners In Praise* 111) or 'Father, Help Your People' (*Partners In Praise* 114). Offering taken while this is sung.

18. Offering is brought forward as the gathering sing 'He is the Way, the end of all my searching' (*Partners In Praise* 115) or 'Father God, I Love You' (*Mission Praise* 56).

19. Recorded music. 'Gloria' (U2, album: *October*; or, with care, using the 'live' version, album *Under Blood Red Sky*). Gathering having risen for 18 (unless already so for 17) remain standing.

20. All say 'Precious claims' (p. 33).
    Someone read 'See the Kingdom' (p. 48).
    All say 'God of listening' (p. 56).

21. Gathering to sit for a moment of quietness.

22. Lights to dim, focus on the cross once more.

23. Recorded music: Philip Bailey, 'Marvellous' (album: *Triumph*).

24. All say the Grace.

Worship 3: The Kingdom is within you

This outline best suits a place where people can come and sit on the floor or kneel. If possible the only light comes from a row of candles. A solitary one burns at the beginning of the service and others are lit while the first music is played.

1. Recorded music: 'Dream Within A Dream', Propoganda (album: *Secret Wish*); or other music that has a mood of space, restlessness, mystery and desire. Follow with: 'On Turning Away', Pink Floyd (album: *A Momentary Lapse of Reason*) and/or either 'Sing Over Me' or 'You Are All In All', Second Chapter of Acts (album: *Far Away Places*).

2. Fade music away.
   Voice: Glorify the Lord with me
          let us together extol his name . . .
          I sought the Lord, and he answered me . . .
          Look to him that you may be radiant with joy,

Taste and see how good the Lord is;
. . . seek peace, and follow after it
. . . no one incurs guilt who takes refuge in him.

Pause.

Voice: This is a service of reflection, of meditation. Many of the words we shall hear come from centuries past. The response in this prayer of extreme beauty from the Nestorian evening office is 'From thee, O Lord'.

Leader: With request and beseeching we ask for the Angel of peace and mercy

Response: From thee, O Lord.

L: Night and day throughout our life, we ask for continued peace for thy Church, and life without sin

R: From thee . . .

L: We ask for continual love, which is the bond of perfectness, with the confirmation of the Holy Spirit

Response

L: We ask for forgiveness of sins and those things which help our lives and please thy Godhead

Response

L: We ask the mercy and compassion of the Lord continually and at all times

Response: From thee, O Lord.

3. We say 'We begin' as on p. 14.
4. We say 'The Lord' (p. 139).
5. Various people read 'What prayer is . . .' (p. 7).
6. Someone asks the gathering to relax and be silent: words from *Contemplative Prayer*, James Borst (Ligouri Publications) p. 51; or say these words, based by Borst on Psalm 34:15:
   'Seek peace and inner silence. Let your mind, heart, will, and feelings become tranquil and serene, let inner storms subside: obsessional thoughts, passionate drives of will and emotions. Seek peace and follow after it.'
7. *Voice:* God alone matters, God, alone is—creation only matters because of Him. 'Wherein does your prayer

consist?' said St John of the Cross to one of his penitents. She replied: 'In considering the Beauty of God, and in rejoicing He has such beauty.'

8. *Another voice:* (words here by Evelyn Underhill, from her spellbinding book *Worship*):
'The great outburst of unshakeable certitude and adoring love which we find upon the lips of the Saints stand up like Alpine peaks in the spiritual landscape of humanity. But the lower pastures, the deepest valleys and darkest forests, even the jungles and the swamps, are all part of the same world; depend on the same given heat and light, the same seasonal vicissitudes. Each in its own way responds to that heat and light, and under its incitement brings forth living things. We shall not understand the mountain by treating it in isolation; nor do justice to the lower levels unless we also remember the heights.'
A different voice: 'God', says St John of the Cross again, 'passes through the thicket of the world, and wherever His glance falls He turns all things to beauty.'

9. Here show slides of the highs and lows of humanity; if there must be music, then jazz is a good form to use, for example *Milestones* by Miles Davis (Fontana).

10. *Voice:* We have seen darkness. (*Extinguish all candles save the last on the end.*)

11. *Voice:* The Light of the World is never extinguished yet for some there seems only darkness. (*Blow out the last remaining lit candle.*)

12. *Voice:* There is a Maronite morning prayer:
'Grant, O Lord, that I may give thee choice gifts; three lighted and dazzling torches; my spirit, my soul and my body. My spirit to the Father, my soul to the Son, my body to the Holy Ghost. O Father, sanctify my spirit! O Son, sanctify my soul! O Holy Ghost, sanctify my sin-soiled body!'
Voice: What shall I say, My God, my Holy Joy!
Voice: Without thy visitation I cannot live!
Voice: The first of the last two thoughts came from St Augustine, the second from Thomas à Kempis.

13. The candles are lit one by one. As they are lit, so the gathering chant 'Jesus Christ, the Light of the World'.

14. Someone to pray 'To encounter the living God' (p. 35), or it could be said together with a leader to keep some pace.

15. Offering.

16. Receipt of offering with saying of 'He is holy' (p. 97).

17. Those who have given the offering to the person receiving shall disperse to set points whether by side pews, central pews, back pews, or by chair rows or appointed areas and there shall lead that group in prayer for the offered needs by the group and these shall take place simultaneously.

18. After due time, the gathering's leader shall say the words 'Lovers of all' (p. 98).

19. All shall say The Lord's Prayer.

20. All shall sing 'Come Holy Ghost, our Souls Inspire' (found in virtually all denominational books, also *Mission Praise* 36).

21. All sit, quiet.

22. Recorded music, 'You are All In All', Second Chapter of Acts. Candles, except central three, extinguished.

Worship 4: Sexuality—human dignity

1. Leader to say 'God for us' (p. 19).

2. Song. *Gentle, Angry People, Songs of Protest & Praise*, p. 13, part two, song 1; or 'That Mighty Resurrected Word' (*Methodist Hymns and Psalms* 658); or 'The Lordship of Christ' (*Partners In Praise* 13); or 'Bless the Lord, O My Soul' (*Mission Praise* 26).

3. Sing 'Jubilate Deo' (Taize chant), or *read* in the form desired Psalm 103 or the Te Deum.

4. Sing 'Bind Us Together, Lord' (*Mission Praise* 21).

5. Say responsively 'God and man and woman' (p. 73).

6. Prayers. Say AIDS (p. 110); say 'Towards a community of men and women' (p. 117).

7. What does it mean to be male, female? Various people

to give their assessment of how it seems to be for (a) magazines; (b) advertising; (c) church; (d) media (TV/radio); (e) film/theatre/art. A number of people speak on their own feelings.

8. Gathering to divide to share their own thoughts and feelings.

9. All come together, singing as they link up once more: 'Teach me To Live' (*Mission Praise* 213).

10. Scripture, read and/or dramatised as thought fit: Isaiah 43:4–7; John 8:3–11; 1 Corinthians 11:11–12; Ephesians 2:14.

11. Further address, or gathering together of group discussions.

Silence . . . silence . . . silence . . .

12. All say 'Standing with him' (p. 53).

13. All to say 'Gender: superfluous' (p. 75).

14. Offering. Offering prayer 'Seek the truth' (p. 108).

15. All sing 'Alleluia Alleluia, give thanks to the Risen Lord' (*Mission Praise* 9, and most recent hymnbooks).

16. All to embrace and share with each other the love of Jesus for all.

17. All to sing 'For I'm Building A People of Power' (*Mission Praise* 50).

18. The Grace together.

Worship 5: Extending or building the Kingdom (1)

1. Recorded music. 'Messiah Man', Ben Okafor (album: *Children of the World*); begin five minutes before service time.

2. Words: said as suggested, 'Lord of all' (p. 16).

3. Song 'To God Be The Glory' (in many denominational hymn books; but add chorus if straight verse lines given, as, for example, in *The Church Hymnary*); or 'Jesus The Name High Over All' (in many church books, or *Mission Praise* 126); or 'Praise With Joy The

World's Creator' (Iona Community worship book).

4. We pray: 'For our sisters and brothers (p. 149); 'Opening' (p. 163); 'God of our daily lives' (p. 163).

5. Statement: 'The kingdom of right relationships' (p. 147).

6. All sing: 'As Water to the thirsty' (*Partners in Praise* 96).

7. All sing: 'One More Step Along The Road' (*Partners in Praise* 97, *Methodist Hymns and Psalms* 746).

8. Stories of the week. (Read the religious press, find relevant positive happenings and tell them, also see other articles which either point out 'need' or 'difficulty'. If possible have a speaker(s); and/or trace major human stories in the local area: and here it should be possible to invite groups/individuals.

9. Specific prayer for persons, situations and conditions mentioned in 8.

10. Read a relevant poem, enact a satirical sketch, show locally-produced art, etc., that relate to 8/9. Or try 'Thirty-seven storey parallel' (p. 151).

11. Someone to read Luke 16:19–21; 1 Corinthians 11:17–22.

12. Reflect on the questions asked in the introduction to the section 'Extending or Building the Kingdom' (p. 137). Do so in the light of 8–10.

13. Recorded music: 'Clap Hands', Tom Waits, from album *Rain Dogs* (Island). Someone to reflect on this song in relation to previous material.

14. Prayer: 'Response' (p. 140).

15. Offering taken during next song: 'If My People, Who Hear My Name' (*New Songs 1987/88*, Kingsway, 11); or 'He Has Showed You, O Man' (*New Songs* 4); or 'When Justice and Peace Kiss' (*Gentle Angry People, Songs of Protest and Praise*).

16. All to say:
    O praise the name of Jesus, our King.
    He calls all.
    Our offerings to Him, our King
    We now give.
    Alleluia.

17. All sing: 'Jesus Christ is waiting, waiting in the Streets' (Iona Community).
18. Grace together.
19. All sing: 'Christ from whom all blessings flow' (in various denominational books; can be located in *Hymns and Psalms*, 764).

Worship 6: Extending or building the Kingdom (2)

Begin the service with silence. Then ask those attending to read through silently Psalm 40. Play U2: '40' (album *War* or *Under Blood Red Sky*).

1. *Opening word:* You are a God of living people.
   Response: You are not ashamed to be our God.
2. *Someone:*   What does it mean to say that we are sharing in the suffering of God?
3. *Someone:*   What does it mean to suffer?
4. *Several readers:* Read relevant extracts from books that deal with suffering and God, as perceived by the sufferer. Do so from a number of angles: (a) political (e.g. something that deals with apartheid); (b) social (e.g. unemployment/poor housing); (c) personal (e.g. *Under The Eye Of The Clock*, Christopher Nolan (published Weidenfeld)); (d) mind (e.g. a case study supplied through Amnesty International). Have the four to six readers on high stools/chairs across the front. Aternatively, invite people who can talk of faith/non-faith in suffering.
5. Someone to sing 'Daughters of Jerusalem' (*Gentle Angry People* 8).
6. Record: a mix of (a) 'Brothers In Arms', Joan Baez, album *Recently* (Gold Castle); (b) 'Biko', Peter Gabriel (single, Virgin/Charisma); (c) 'System of Survival', Earth, Wind & Fire, album *Touch the World* (CBS); (d) 'How Can We Ease The Pain', Maxi Priest, album *Maxi* (10 Records); (e) 'South Africa', Working Week, album *Companeros* (Virgin); (f) 'The Hungry Night',

Sheila Walsh, album *Shadowlands* (Myrrh); (g) 'I'm Gon' Stand', 'We All . . . Everyone Of Us', Sweet Honey In The Rock, album *We All . . . Everyone Of Us* (Flying Fish Records). Obviously there are many other tracks that might be listed.

Alternatively: a folk singer to sing songs with gathering participation, prefacing each song with its social/political/personal etc. background.

7. The Lord's Prayer.
8. Scripture reading: Lamentations 1:1–7; Luke 23:26–31; Revelation 21:1–8.
9. Add comment.
10. Christians sharing in the suffering of God. Give thanks for the work of particular Christian concerns or individuals and cover as wide a field as possible.
11. Sing as a gathering, or soloist with chorus, 'A Touching Place' (Iona Community); or all sing the hymn 'Sweet Is The Work, My God, My King' (found in most collections); or have both.
12. Sing 'The Broken Body' (Iona Community) and possibly let sections of the gathering take particular verses; or, from the same source, 'Shake Up The Morning'.
13. Read: 'A World Without Tears' along the gathering (as found in *At All Times and in All Places*, pp. 79ff.); or, from the same source, read with gathering response as outlined 'Truth', pp. 41ff.
14. Record: 'Exodus', Bob Marley and The Wailers (album: *Babylon By Bus*, Island Records); or 'Child of the Universe', Barclay James Harvest (album *Concert for the People*, Polydor Records).
15. All sing: 'My Soul Doth Magnify The Lord' (*Mission Praise* 159). All Sing: 'Sing We The King' (many denominational hymn books, *Mission Praise* 206).
16. Grace.
17. Play again '40' from U2.

Worship 7: Living in the Kingdom (1)

Preface the worship gathering by playing material from Jesus Music albums such as Leon Patillo, *Love Around The World* (Myrrh); The Clark Sisters, *Heart and Soul* (Rejoice/Word); The Inspirational Choir, *Higher and Higher* (here, play the title track or 'Sweet Inspiration'). The first named albums have shorter track times, so select several songs. Begin this process three or four minutes before those who shall lead the worship gathering enter. Previously, have someone playing on piano, string instruments, etc., a variety of new Christian praise material.

Have the walls and the entrance area of the worship gathering covered with pictures, posters and written explanation that illustrate the theme of Living in the Kingdom. (See Introduction to this part of the book, p. 158.) Obviously use of some video players would not go amiss.

Encourage people to come forty-five minutes before the worship time. Have some tea, coffee, soft drinks and sandwiches for those who come.

At various points in the church/hall have exhibitions from Christian and charitable organisations. If possible see if someone from the group can be present. Also have display material from local 'helpline' and 'advice' bodies, e.g. the Samaritans, Citizens' Advice Bureau; and some form of general survey that will cover all the 'services' that are available.

1. As the chosen music ends, invite the gathering to stand.
2. Read responsively 'God is alive' (p. 20).
3. Read: 'A morning prayer of the Kingdom' (p. 31); or (if evening) 'To encounter the living God' (p. 35).
4. All sing 'All Hail the Power of Jesus' Name' (in virtually all denominational books; *Mission Praise* 5); or 'I Will Enter His Gates' (*Mission Praise* 97); or 'Praise to the Lord, the Almighty' (again, in most collections; *Mission Praise* 192).
5. 'Power of the Spirit' (p. 39: see note at the end of this extract).

6. One or several people say 'The all-embracing Spirit' (p. 42).

7. Read responsively The Magnificat. (If denominational hymn books are used, for example *Methodist Hymns and Psalms*, it is so set out that it can easily be used in this way. If not, then have various voices read.)

8. Scripture: Isaiah 61:1-3; Luke 4:16-21.

9. Solo: 'Which One Is Which' by Sydney Carter (*Partners In Praise* 33); or 'Said Judas to Mary' by Sydney Carter (*Partners in Praise* 66).

10. Here, choose several people from whatever groups you wish to speak about their work. A Christian and a non-Christian would make an interesting mix, for who said care is the province of Christians or religious people?

11. Questions and brief discussion.

12. Have someone young read 'We are invited' (p. 164).

13. If possible form a procession around the building and stop briefly at each point for a short word/message/explanation, and prepared prayer. At each point sing a verse from 'As Your Family Lord' (see *Methodist Hymns and Psalms* 595).

14. Prayers: of confession. Read 'Prayers of confession' (p. 166).

15. Ask for open prayer with concentration on the work that is shown and displayed.

16. A period of silence. The silence to be interspersed with someone reminding the gathering of various needs in the community.

17. All sing: 'The Earth is the Lord's' (*Songs of Gentle Angry People* 51); or 'Thy Loving Kindness' (*Mission Praise* 241); or 'O For A Thousand Tongues'; or 'Jesus, Lover Of My Soul' (both are found in virtually all denominational books; *Mission Praise* 168 and 120 respectively).

18. A short address—biblical exposition; or 'People Can Be People' (*At All Times and In All Places* pp. 140ff.).

19. Offering for causes mentioned or for one specific cause.

20. As offering is taken gathering can sing 'How Good is the God We Adore' (*Mission Praise* 77); or, as in some books,

'This, this is the God We Adore'. The verses can be repeated according to the time taken to take the offering.

21. When the offering has been blessed, all shall sing the refrain of 'O Come let Us Adore Him' (*Mission Praise* 165).

22. Say the Benedictions give in *At All Times and In All Places*, p. 161, along rows.

23. By rows repeat 21, and then as a gathering sing.

Worship 8: Living in the Kingdom (2)

As has been said previously, allow some three to four minutes of the first music item mentioned to be heard in a worship context.

1. Recorded music 'Heaven Is 10 Zillion Light Years Away', Paul Johnson (album *Paul Johnson*, CBS).

2. Half a dozen readers for 'Worship happening' (p. 10) reading fairly quickly, each reader reading words until the dots.

3. Gathering stands and reads responsively 'The One who will' (p. 177).

4. *Voice:* But what are the needs within society? Where is there real giving, receiving, sharing and good relationships?

5. Recorded music: (a) the verse in Paul Simon's song, 'Blessed', that begins 'Blessed is the land' and ends, 'O Lord, why have you forsaken me?' (b) Follow 'Blessed' immediately with 'Sounds of Silence' by Paul Simon. ('Blessed' is found on the album *Sounds Of Silence* (CBS); 'Sounds of Silence' can be found in various forms, in early style, the self-titled album, *The Graduate, Simon and Garfunkel's Greatest Hits* (all CBS), *The Concert In Central Park* (Geffen).) Alternatively, having the songs sung by someone.

6. Some people to give flesh to the questions asked in 4.

Both positive and negative, in terms of the local area and the church.

7. Reading: a number of people to read the text of Chapter 17 of John Smith's *On The Side Of The Angels* (Lion) to the end of first paragraph, p. 236.

8. A time of silence.

9. Say 'Opening' (p. 163).

10. Someone to read 'Universals' (p. 161).

11. Turn lights slowly down; as this is done, bring up the track 'A Love Supreme', Will Downing (album: *Will Downing*, Island Records). Play the music in the darkness and stillness. As track fades, bring up lights (or light candles) with someone saying:
    Will Downing says on the back of his record sleeve: 'To God. For blessing me with whatever talent I possess. All praise belongs to You, for without You I am nothing.'
    The song is by jazz musician John Coltrane—arguably one of the most powerful spiritual statements to emerge from the jazz tradition. It can exist as a simple love song, a love song offered up to the Almighty.

12. *Voice:* So we come to a time of praise, Scripture and prayer, still aware of giving, receiving, sharing and good relationships.

13. Someone to sing: 'Jesus Take Me As I Am' (*Mission Praise* 127).

14. All to sing: 'Spirit of the Living God' (*Mission Praise* 209).

15. All to sing: 'Father, We Adore You' (*Mission Praise* 44).

16. All to sing: 'From the Rising of the Sun' (*Mission Praise* 54).

17. Someone to read 'God and me' (p. 11).

18. Someone to read 'One with the Father' (p. 26); or to share readings.

19. All to read and make responses as given for 'All to Him' (p. 25).

20. All say 'So marvellous' (p. 36).

21. Scripture readings: Isaiah 40:21–31; John 6:1–13; 1 Corinthians 13.

22. Giving, receiving, sharing—good relationships in terms of God, His caring, His loving, His giving, His commands. A short address/exposition. At its completion, speaker to invite comment from the gathering.
23. A call to pray for . . .
24. A call for testimony . . .
25. A call for commitment, dedication . . .
26. A time of silence: leading to a time of song (as asked), and of witness, as felt and led by the Spirit.
27. A 'dance' of joy to 'A love supreme' (p. 221).
28. All to stand and say The Lord's Prayer.
29. To sit, the offering to be taken, to sing 'Majesty' (*Mission Praise* 151).
30. To rise and sing 'Sing Alleluia' (*Mission Praise* 204).

Worship 9: Journey, future, second coming, end— the Kingdom past, present and future (1)

1. In silence, eight people shall walk forward, and read Psalm 96 (RSV) in the following manner:
   Verse 1: two men and two women from 'O sing' to 'all the earth!'
   Verse 2: add two further men, two women from 'Sing to the Lord' to 'day to day'.
   Verse 3: all eight say 'Declare his glory . . . all the peoples!'
   Verse 4: one woman says 'For great . . . greatly to be praised'.
   Verse 4: one man says 'He is to . . . above all gods'.
   Verse 5: two of the readers say 'For all the gods . . . Lord made the heavens'.
   Verse 6: further one man, one woman to make four voices saying 'Honour and majesty . . . before him'.
   Verse 6: add further man, woman to make six voices saying 'Strength and beauty . . . in his sanctuary'.
   Verse 7: add two remaining voices to make eight, saying 'Ascribe . . . of the peoples'.
   Verse 8: 'ascribe . . . due to his name;'

Verse 8: one woman says 'Bring an offering . . . his courts!'

Verse 9: one woman says 'Worship . . . in holy array;'

Verse 9: 'tremble . . . all the earth!'

Verse 10: add one man to two women, saying 'say among the nations . . . Lord reigns!'

Verse 10: add one woman, one man making four, saying 'yea the world . . . it shall never be moved'.

Verse 10: add remaining four voices, saying 'he will judge . . . let the sea roar'

Verse 11: 'and all that fills it'.

Verse 12: two women say 'let the fields . . in it!'

Verse 12: two men say 'Then shall the . . . joy before'

Verse 13: '. . . for he comes'.

Verse 13: two men and two women, making four, say 'for he comes to judge the earth'

Verse 13: all eight voices say 'he will judge . . . with his truth'.

2. All sing: 'Lo he comes with clouds descending' (found in most books; *Mission Praise* 141).

3. All say: 'In Christ' (p. 196).

4. All say: 'Affirmation' (p. 189).

5. All say: 'Constant welcome' (p. 170).

6. Record: 'To Every Generation', Debby Boone (album: *Friends for Life*).

7. All say: text of song heard, 'To Every Generation' (p. 169).

8. All sing: 'Rejoice The Lord Is King' (found in most hymn books; *Mission Praise* 195).

9. Prayers: say responsively The Benedictus (see for instance *Methodist Hymns and Psalms* 825).

10. Say responsively 'Saviour of the World' (*Methodist Hymns and Psalms* 829).

11. Sing: 'Hark what a sound' (in most hymn books); or, 'There's a Light Upon the Mountains'.

12. All say Revelation 4:11: 'Worthy art thou, our Lord and our God, to receive the glory and the honour and the power: for thou didst create all things, and because of thy will they were, and were created.'

13. All women to say: 'Grant unto us with one heart and one mouth to glorify and magnify thy glorious and majestic Name!'

14. All men to say: as for 13.

15. The two halves of the gathering to face each other and say together: 'Grant unto us with one heart and one mouth to glorify and magnify thy glorious and majestic Name!'

16. Solo: 'O Lord My God' (*Mission Praise* 173). (All shall sing the refrain on verse 4, otherwise refrain shall be sung by the three thirds of the gathering so divided.)

17. Solo: verse of 'O what a gift!'; all shall sing refrain. (In various hymn books; *Mission Praise* 176.)

18. A number of people shall read chosen Scripture verses that speak of His Coming in Glory.

19. Address.

20. Small singing group: 'We See The Lord' (*Mission Praise* 257).

21. All shall sing: 'We really want to thank You' (*Mission Praise* 256).

22. The Lord's Prayer.

23. The Offering. (Pianist might play a selection of hymns/songs that speak of His coming.)

24. During and after receipt of offering 'Mine Eyes Have Seen' shall be sung (most hymn books, with refrain).

25. One person says
'We look for His coming but meantime there is much work to be done', then all say 'Commitment' (*At All Times and In All Places*, pp. 100–1).

Worship 10: Journey, future, second coming, end—the Kingdom, past, present and future (2)

Arrange a display that gives some impression of the Church down the ages from the first century onwards. Chart the major happenings. Feature the main figures. Let there be a special section devoted to the present century especially the Church and Evangelism, Women and the Church, Change

in Missionary Emphasis, Church Unity, Race, Church and
Social-Political Matters, etc.

Show visually how churches and chapels have changed in
outside and internal design.

Try and represent the Church of tomorrow—in this be
bold and adventurous, even at the risk of seeming a little
ridiculous.

1. One part of the gathering to sing 'O God our Help In
   Ages Past'. Another to sing 'O God Of Bethel'. Another
   to sing, on their completion, 'Deep In The Shadows'
   (see *Methodist Hymns and Psalms* 447); and a further 'We
   Come Unto Our Father's God' (like the first two
   named, found in most denominational hymn books.
   Sing a number of verses rather than the whole).
2. All say: 'Lord we praise you' (p. 192).
3. All sing: 'God, Your Glory We Have Seen' (see
   Methodist Hymns and Psalms 459).
4. In procession around the church (outside if an area
   where this has point and purpose) sing from the
   following: 'For The Might of Thine Arm', 'Through
   The Night Of Doubt and Sorrow', 'Soldiers of Christ
   Arise', 'As Jacob with travel' (see *Methodist Hymns and
   Psalms* 444).
5. Embrace each other and whisper the peace.
6. Say the traditional words of Adoration/Thanksgiving/
   Forgiveness, as found in the service of Morning Prayer.
7. Let lights be dimmed, candles lit, explode with joy and
   sing one or more of the Alleluias from Taize or use
   accordingly from the Taize cassettes that are easily
   obtainable from religious shops.
8. Say 'Litany of the saints' (p. 194). Adapt as thought fit.
9. Say 'A litany of intercession' (p. 92).
10. Scripture: Hebrews 11:1—12:2. (Use different voices.
    Let all say the verses of 12:1, 2.)
11. Scripture: John 1:35–50; Acts 2:1–13, 22–24.
12. All sing: 'A Safe Stronghold our God is Still' (in most
    hymn books); or, as in some books, use 'A Mighty

Fortress Is Our God'; or, if numbers are small and Ein Feste Burg is found a trifle arduous, 'The Lord Is My Strength' (*Mission Praise* 225); or 'Arm of the Lord Awake' (most hymn books).

13. All gather in circles—look at each other—give welcome by eye-contact—recognising the need within us all, the brokenness of each for which the Spirit was given, to heal and to invest with all power. Give thanks as led. Pray that all might know and trust the Spirit moving among us to empower and to heal, that this gathering might increasingly become a community of Christ.

14. It would be good if in simple fashion all should receive bread and wine with the basic words of the Lord's Supper/Communion, or whatever name is used. To sing: the song 'Jesus Said I Am The Bread Of Life' (found in many modern collections) and/or 'Let Us Break Bread' (found accordingly). If space is free, the gathering will have circled several tables that have bread and wine. (If at all possible avoid those silly individual communion cups.)

15. Silence.

16. Sing: 'O Lord hear My Prayer' from Taize; or hear, and sing with the recorded cassette.

17. Pray for the experience of the Spirit moving in our daily lives, in our ordinary needs and activities. Be so honest that it seems embarrassing as well as delightful.

18. Someone to remind all that as the children of God, we have the ability to act, for the Spirit has been poured out on us all; poured, not meted out.

19. Sing: 'He Is Here' (*Mission Praise* 68); or 'Go Forth and Tell' (*Mission Praise* 61); or 'For I'm Building' (*Mission Praise* 50).

20. Have three proclaimers/preachers: each shall read some famous or powerful words; e.g., one could say those words of Dr Martin Luther King's famous address (*At All Times and In All Places*, p. 68).

21. All say 'Litany of new birth' (p. 198).

22. Sing all or part of 'For all the Saints' (in most church books).

23. Say 'God of all' (p. 19).
24. Sing: 'All People That On Earth Do Dwell' (in almost all church hymn books, note descant).
25. Shout from row to row 'Praise the Lord'. Finally, all shout 'Hallelujah!'

Resources: Books and Music

Books

This is a list of books where there will be found very useful material. It is a source guide and not an attempt to list an exhaustive, far-reaching coverage of worship material. It mentions only a few of the many prayer manuals that are available.

ARM (Alliance of Radical Methodists): *Gentle Angry People*, available from 92 Bodmin Avenue, Weeping Cross, Stafford ST17 0EQ.

Bailey, Gordon: a number of books, offering a wide variety of poetry/satire. *Plastic World, Patchword Quilt*; *I Want To Tell You How I Feel, God*. Compiler of *100 Contemporary Christian Poets* (Lion).

BBC: *Pocket Praise*.

Bible Society: 'Creative Resources' series.

Blyth, Myra and Jasper, Tony: *At All Times And In All Places* (Marshall Pickering).

Bowater, Chris: *Creative Worship* (Marshall Pickering).

Brand, Leslie: series of meditations on biblical books, well-suited to creative worship services. (Concordia).

Castle, Tony: *Tomorrow's People* (Mayhew McCrimmon).

Church of Scotland Department of Education: 'Together' series.

Fellingham, Dave: *Worship Restored* (Kingsway).

Field, Paul: *Breaking Bread* (Kingsway).

Fisherfolk: constant stream of creative material, via Celebration Services.

Francis, Leslie: *A Feast Of Words* (Collins).

Frost, Brian: *Come Celebration*, a wide assortment of often illuminating material, particularly good on forgiveness, peace, friendship. From author at 35 Buckingham Palace Gate, London SW1.

Gjerding I. and Kinnamon K: *No Longer Strangers* (WCC).

Henderson, Stewart: *Fan Male* (Stride Publications), *Assembled In Britain* (Marshall Pickering), interviews from *Strait* that might prove useful for quotation etc., *Adrift in the 80's* (ed. Henderson, Marshall Pickering).

Iona Community: excellent worship resource material, The Abbey, Iona, Argyle, PA76 6SN.

Jasper, Tony: *Living Words for Now* (SPCK); *Thank God* (Lion).

John Paul, The Preacher Press: under this imprint a range of often stimulating material.

Jones, E. S. P.: *Worship And Wonder* (Galliard).

Kairos Group: *Jesus Is Alive* (Falcon).

King, Joe: *Leading Worship* (Kingsway) for instrumentalists and singers.

Mallison, John: *Creative Ideas for Small Groups* (Renewal, Australia, can be located in Britain).

Micklem, Caryl: *More Contemporary Prayers* (SCM).

Morley, J. and Ward, H.: *Contemporary Women*. From MOW, Napier Hall, Hide Place, Vincent Street, London SW1P 4NJ. Like *No More Strangers*, excellent material from women writers.

Oosterhuis, Huub: *Your Word is Near* (Fowler Wright).

St Andrews Press: *New Ways to Worship*.

Shea, John: *The Hour of the Unexpected* (Argus).

Sojourners Community: *New People, I Am Your Security* (P.O. Box 29272, Washington DC 20017, USA).

Stevenson, Geoffrey and Judith: *Steps of Faith* (Kingsway).

Stickley, Steve and Janet: *Footnotes* (Hodder).

Turner, Steve: variety of material, all warmly recommended

WCC: *The Kingdom On Its Way*.

General sources:

Amnesty International, British Section, 5 Roberts Place, London EC1 0EJ.

Christian Aid, P.O. Box 1, London SW9 8BH.

Corrymeela, Corrymeela House, 8 Upper Crescent, Belfast BT7 1NT.

Church Pastoral Aid Society (CPAS), Falcon Court, 32 Fleet Street, London EC47 1DB.

Iona Community, as previously given, or Pearce Institute, Govan Cross, Glasgow, G52.

Methodist Division of Education and Youth, 2 Chester House, Pages Lane, Muswell Hill, London N10 1PR.

Quaker Home Service, Friends House, Euston Road, London NW1 2BJ.

Scripture Union, 230 City Road, London EC1.

Major denominational bodies and house-movement based organisations issue considerable material. For example, the Fellowship of United Reformed Youth issue *Image*, a study-kit worship project. Diocesan Youth, Church of Ireland Youth Council, at CIYC, 65 Fitzwilliam Square, Dublin 2, S. Ireland, have a worship pack with young people especially in mind. For creative praise material: Glyndley Manor, Stone Cross, Eastbourne, East Sussex BN24 5BS.

Music

Since our suggested recorded music list in *At All Times And In All Places* met a positive response we have ventured forth again. It is not a question of entertaining anyone, but rather to see how the 'worship' framework that was set out in the introduction can receive some input from popular music.

At the risk of boring or being repetitive, it must be stated that recorded music may not always aid 'informal' worship, it may not make people more aware, and in the wrong hands, given bad acoustics, a poor sound system, a duff cassette player with volume output reaching no more than a few rows of chair or pews, a badly taped recording or a record track chosen partially or completely incorrectly, it can be a lethal dose of bad spiritual medicine. And there are other dangers.

At best, however, it can aid a mood, a feeling, heighten already roused sensitivity, bring more sharply into focus a theme/meditation/address, lead listeners into a greater awareness of spiritual and biblical truth: a succinct song lyric and tune that may be derived from someone's Christian orientation, as obviously with U2, may well be capturing a dimension of faith and expressing it in a form that makes especial sense to people reared in this pop-culture age.

'Live' groups or bands seem more of hindrance than a help, given the setting for most worship gatherings. Obviously when the participants have a high degree of musical awareness, competence and professionalism then their output can be harnessed in worthy fashion. It is likely that the only truly positive settings will be festivals and large sized gatherings. There is no time within a planned worship gathering for a pop group to try and assemble its sound, to run annoying wires everywhere, to have roadies dashing to and fro, amps blowing, guitars out of tune, mics popping or going dead, and so on.

That said, there are obvious plus factors in other kinds of musical forms, whether it be an orchestra, a string quartet, a jazz group, a folk group or artist, or singing that is led by acoustic guitar.

But we cannot offer guidance here for we do not know the competence of whoever might be regaling obviously unknown gatherings! To a degree we can offer commentary and advice on popular recordings and we are assuming the right setting, a high standard sound system, and professionalism on the part of operators.

There have been many impressive albums since the list of material that was printed in *At All Times And In All Places* (pp. 170ff.). This new list is suggestive rather than definitive. There should be people within any gathering who can advise on particularly good tracks from the albums we list, although some of these are taken and looked at more closely in the ensuing text.

For the most part we would suggest that each album on our list has possibilities. To some degree the level of appreciation—if any—can be gleaned by establishing within a worship group a number of people who would have the task of seeing what particular songs and tunes were suited to certain occasions.

At the risk of being heavy-handed, it seems important to reiterate a point made elsewhere. Little is achieved by us or anyone dictating, or attempting to relate general advice to a specific case. We do not know the composition of your gathering, its musical tastes and awareness. And should you be someone unversed in contemporary music and perhaps hoping that we might lead you into the inner sanctum of foolproof success then we humbly suggest that you forget the whole affair, for you are likely to miss the right nuances and innocently stumble into a minefield. There are few records and few artists who embrace a very wide public. Today, more than ever in pop music's history from 1955 onwards, there are diversified fields and each attracts its own clientele. Music must be seen in relation to a chosen theme, prayer or meditative word. Left to itself, it might well seem as though it is being used to favour a particular grouping within your mixed gathering, and may well isolate others; and in a teenage setting the wrong choice can even produce a mild form of ridicule, and disbelief that anyone could conceivably play so-and-so; and it matters not that the artist or group sells records by the million worldwide. The major exception to this might rest in someone's saying that a particular piece of music is important to them because it relates to their own life, experience or religious awareness.

At all times, use of music should be prefaced by a whole series of questions: does the music envisaged glorify God? If so, in what way? If not, then in what way can it qualify as useful in terms of worship? What is it saying about man/woman, about the world, about behaviour and attitudes? In practical terms, can the lyrics be heard/deciphered, are they readily understandable? Is the verse clear of profanity? Is there another song that might be used, why this one and not that? If we are using a number of musical forms, do they blend? Are they arranged in the right order? If music is used to 'assault', to 'provoke' then are there ways in which it will threaten rather than aid?

These are questions which should be addressed to each and every element that is considered for worship, but perhaps in even greater intensity here than in any other area. No time should be given to music if the overall aim is 'attracting' people; the use of it may well do so, but if the underlying motivation is this then it is more than likely the eventual presentation will be an embarrassment. In any case, the idea of music is not to lead people into buying records the next day at their local record store, it is to make clear the Gospel, to present an insight or further awareness, to help people into a better understanding of themselves that goes beyond mere surface level. There is no argument for playing music for the purposes of keeping young people interested. The very reasoning behind this is suspect. In any case it suggests that those so worried have little idea themselves as to why young people should bother. Further, it is unacceptable that music should be featured because it has been suggested by enthusiastic persons who are so engrossed in their likes that they themselves have not thought out the 'whys' and 'wherefores'. The use of contemporary music should be made with care, great care.

Suggested albums:
The Christians, The Christians (Island).
Popped In Souled Out, Wet Wet Wet (Precious/Phonogram).
Bad, Michael Jackson (Epic: track 'Mirror in the Bathroom' with its theme of 'I want a changed life')
Graceland, Paul Simon (WB).
A Momentary Lapse of Reason, Pink Floyd (EMI: tracks 'Signs of Life', 'On The Turning Away', 'Sorrow').
The Joshua Tree, U2 (Island).
Always Guaranteed, Cliff Richard (EMI).

No Jacket Required, Phil Collins (Virgin).

Solitude Standing, Suzanne Vega (A&M).

Maxi, Maxi Priest (10 Records: particularly the track 'How Can We Ease The Pain').

Destiny's Song, Courtney Pine (instrumental, track: 'Sunday'; Island Records).

Savage, Eurythmics (RCA: tracks 'Shame', 'Savage', 'Brand New Day').

Say So, Sheila Walsh (Myrrh).

The Turning, Leslie Phillips (Myrrh).

One Faith, One Lord, One Baptism, Aretha Franklin (Arista).

Echo and the Bunneymen, Echo and the Bunneymen (tracks: 'New Direction', 'All My Life', 'All In Your Mind', 'Bombers Fly By').

Masque, Manfred Mann's Earth Band (10: track 'Hymn').

Touch The World, Earth, Wind & Fire ('System of Survival', 'Evil Roy'; CBS).

Jam Packed, Steve Arrington (EMI: tracks 'Stone Love', 'True Love Always').

I'm Grateful, Garth Hewitt (Myrrh).

Decisions, The Winans (Q-West).

Tango In The Night, Fleetwood Mac (Warner Brothers: track 'Family Man').

Sirius, Clannad (RCA: tracks 'Second nature', 'Something To Believe In', 'Many Roads').

Triumph, Philip Bailey (Myrrh).

Friends for Life, Debby Boone (Lamb).

Recently, Joan Baez (Gold Castle: tracks 'Let Us Break Bread', 'Oh Freedom', 'Biko', 'Brothers In Arms').

Shake Zulu, Ladysmith Mambazo (Warner Brothers).

The Wild Frontier, Randy Stonehill (Myrrh).

Against The Grain, Altar Boys (Frontline).

Wendy and Lisa, Wendy and Lisa (Virgin).

Soul Survivor, Al Green (A&M).

All Systems Go, Donna Summer (WEA: tracks 'Voices In The Night', 'Dinner with Gershwin', 'Bad Reputation').

Higher and Higher, Inspirational Choir (Portrait).

The Search Is Over, Tramaine (A&M).

The Wonders Of His Love, Philip Bailey (Myrrh).

Change, David Grant (Polydor).

Paul Johnson, Paul Johnson (CBS: particularly 'Heaven Is Zen Million Miles Away', 'Every Kinda People').

This Is The Sea, The Waterboys (Island: track 'Spirit').

Feel Something Drawing Me On, Sweet Honey In The Rock (Making Waves).

Children Of The World, Ben Okafor (Ears & Eyes).

We All . . . Everyone Of Us, Sweet Honey In The Rock (Flying Fish).

Doo-Be-Doo-Wop bop!, Take Six (Reprise).

The Lion and the Cobra, Sinead O'Connor (Chrysalis: track 'Jerusalem').

Der Kommissar, After The Fire (CBS: tracks 'Joy', 'Dancing In The Shadows', '1980-F', 'Laser Love', 'One Rule For You').

Poetic Champions Compose, Van Morrison (Mercury: tracks 'Give Me My Rapture', 'Did Ye Get Healed?' 'I Forgot That Love Existed', 'Sometimes I Feel Like A Motherless Child').

The Whole Story, Kate Bush (EMI: tracks 'Cloudbursting', 'The Man With The Child In His Eyes', 'Breathing', 'Running Up That Hill').

Magnetic Heaven, Wax (RCA: tracks 'Hear No Evil', 'Only A Visitor').

Rain Dogs, Tom Waits (Island: track 'Clap Hands').

The World Won't Listen, The Smiths (Rough Trade: tracks 'The Boy With The Thorn In His Side', 'Unlovable').

Viva Hate, Morrissey (EMI: tracks 'Everyday Is Like Sunday', 'Break Up The Family', 'Angel, Angel Down We Go Together').

Far Away Places, Second Chapter of Acts (Live Oak).

Using Music

How can music be used? This is a difficult question to answer since so much depends on the 'basics' already listed but now repeated: place, colour, acoustics, shape of building/room, ambience, sound system employed, sound

operators, make-up of gathering in age and style and the
theme that has been chosen.

But here are a number of practical suggestions:

1. With taste and sensitivity, play music while people are
gathering. This can merely set a mood; or, by using a
printed information sheet or service order, music titles can
be given, with explanations for its use in relation to the
theme or some aspect of the worship framework (e.g.
adoration). The gathering can be asked to sit with eyes
closed, or to kneel, to be silent, to meditate via a prayer you
have given.

2. Intersperse prayers or readings with appropriate music:
here, the music theme must be spot-on and it should be
brought quietly up as the reader is finishing his/her words so
there is no disquieting gap or silence in which the gathering
may well conclude 'all is over' and awaken their senses once
more!

3. Use verses (or just the words spoken by someone) as a
means of reflection—prayer. To take an example, Queen's
'Another One Bites The Dust' might be played: but
counteract their thoughts with the words of Jesus, or of how
'God so loved . . .'

4. Let someone reflect with musical illustration on what
seems to be coming through in the current music world and
add commentary that seems apt from a Christian perspective. This can be part of a series in which during worship
people are asked to hear and reflect. The themes developed
might then lead to prayers . . .

5. When there is an obvious 'Christian' feel and sensitivity
then the music can be played in its own right.

6. You might run a number of services during which you
will feature what Christians are saying and doing in the arts
and communication areas. It might well be that you could
feature the work of Christians in the secular music world. I
did this once at a youth service, for six of the singles I had to
review for a magazine just happened to be by Christians.

7. Play bursts of different music interspersed with silence
and spoken word, on a chosen theme. Here the music

volume must be sensitive and the 'lighting' sympathetic to the overall mood.

8. You might have a featurette on a Christian artist and conceivably gain an interview with this person.

9. Obviously you can end a worship gathering by playing appropriate music.

You might have use of a video and can add an important visual element with the right tape.

Do not be afraid to explore the 'resources' which are there in most gatherings, for it would be surprising to find that music was not very much to the fore in most people's lives.

The list of records and suggested tracks is no more than a guide and is in no way presented as some kind of authoritative statement. Meanwhile the music world pushes ahead relentlessly!

Other Marshall Pickering Paperbacks

ISSUES FACING CHRISTIANS TODAY

John Stott

A major appraisal of contemporary social, moral, sexual and global issues, combined with one man's attempt to think 'Christianly' on this broad spectrum of complex questions, make ISSUES FACING CHRISTIANS TODAY a *best-seller*.

'This is powerful stuff. Highly contemporary . . . awkwardly personal . . . thoroughly biblical.' *Baptist Times*

'A valuable resource for Christians responding to the huge needs to seek the renewal of society.' *Buzz*

'It stands alone as a scholarly, scriptural and profoundly well-argued and researched authority on many of the most perplexing and intractable problems of the present day.' *Renewal*

THE INFINITE GUARANTEE: A Meditation on the Last Words from the Cross

Andrew Cruickshank

A profound and thoughtful series of reflections on Jesus' seven sayings from the Cross by one of TV's most familiar and favourite actors. Andrew Cruickshank's deeply challenging study provides ideal devotional reading material, which encourages us to establish their significance of Jesus' words for us today.

'. . . a very remarkable book . . . quite outstanding. It demands to be read, re-read and read again. I can only describe it as *a little masterpiece . . .*' Rev Dr William Neil

TWO MILLION SILENT KILLINGS: the Truth about Abortion

Dr Margaret White

Essential, informed reading for all Christians on this critical contemporary issue; likely to engender wholehearted and healthy controversy.

GP Margaret White exposes the deliberate attempt to confuse the public over the issue of abortion by the use of euphemistic language and the minimizing of its harmful side-effects. She traces the history of abortion from legal, medical and religious perspectives, describes the clinical methods used to terminate pregnancies, and answers the various arguments put forward by the pro-abortionists in terms of God's basic rules for life. At the heart of these is the Creator's desire for his creation's health, stability and well-being. Dr White demonstrates that the extent of the damaging effects of abortion on women and society is one of today's best-kept secrets.

THE GOSPEL COMMUNITY

John Tiller

An important and timely call to the established churches to rediscover the distinctive life of the Spirit and to become true 'gospel communities' – attractive, authoritative and relevant.

Neither the experience of renewal nor nationwide evangelistic missions resulted in a mass return to the churches. Instead, the house church seems to promise a better future for Christianity. Can revival still come through the established churches? John Tiller, Chancellor and Canon Residentiary of Hereford Cathedral, looks at Jesus' radical definitions of the temple, priesthood and sacrifice, and outlines the style of leadership which will enable the church to become again a 'living temple'. A critical book practically showing the way ahead for the established church.

CHOICES . . . CHANGES

Joni Eareckson Tada

Joni has inspired millions with her courage and faith in dealing with her quadriplegia. In her third book, she writes revealingly of her life, her ministry and her marriage. 'I've sat in on bridal showers for so many others; it seems odd that it should be my turn. In my wheelchair with its dusty gears and squeaky belts, I seem slightly out of place among the delicately wrapped gifts and dainty finger sandwiches.'

This warm, honest, sometimes funny and often poignant autobiography shows us vividly that though life is full of changes – wanted and unwanted – God uses each one of them to make us more like Him. Illustrated.

EYES THAT SEE: The Spiritual Gift of Discernment

Douglas McBain

The first of a new series, Renewal Issues in the Church, which examines the effects of charismatic renewal on corporate church life and individual Christian experience from a biblical perspective.

Douglas McBain, a leading figure in renewal first in the Baptist Church and now on a wider basis, provides a comprehensive and thorough scripture-based guide to the gift of discernment; which, with the resurgence of emphasis on signs and wonders, healing and deliverance, is 'the most necessary gift for the present day church'.

If you wish to receive *regular information* about *new books*, please send your name and address to:

London Bible Warehouse
PO Box 123
Basingstoke
Hants RG23 7NL

Name..

Address.................................... ....

....

....

....

I am especially interested in:
- ☐ Biographies
- ☐ Fiction
- ☐ Christian living
- ☐ Issue related books
- ☐ Academic books
- ☐ Bible study aids
- ☐ Children's books
- ☐ Music
- ☐ Other subjects